Too Much Coffee Man's™

Parade of Tirade

by

SHANNON WHEELER

INTRODUCTION

by HENRY ROLLINS

How many times have you sat alone in a coffee house and stared into the liquid black abyss of your coffee cup to see the blasted reflection of your own mortal futility staring back at you as you sit still while being jettisoned towards the end of your life? Your thoughts ricochet like wild bullets fired into an iron-walled room. Getting older. Every day closer to death. Never took advantage of your youth. Squandered your resources. Old relationships come back to haunt you as you reference them against the one you're trapped in now or the one you wish you were. Your obsessions scream and taunt you from the corners of your eyes. Your thoughts smash down like a neural hammer on your cranial anvil. One thing becomes clear as you look at the tables full of people chattering away like dolphins on speed—only the strong dare to drink from the bottomless black insomnia mother pool alone. That would be you.

Like a Hopper painting, the coffee house sits like a lit oasis in the desolate nocturnal city sprawl. Inside is hope and respite from your headlong pitch into oblivion. The first cup makes sense. The second makes more. On you go. As you pick up speed, everything around you seems to slow down slightly. Perfection. You are now traveling at life's frantic and banal velocity. The canvas of another night shot full of holes. The slow commute back to the room to wait it out until you are released from the teeth and cast into twitching sleep: never deep and never long as your mind slams down the rails. The sun comes up; the noise level skyrockets as the city lurches forward with metal-on-metal desperation.

Too Much Coffee Man is the embodiment of our stressed urban intellectual overload smashing into a wall. He sits, grinding his teeth in the eye of the storm, deeply entrenched in the battlefield of our collective fears and neurosis. As you pass your days in that job you hate, as you pummel yourself into distraction from the excruciating reality that it's all slipping away, Too Much Coffee Man is on point, doing . . . well, not much of anything to qualify as a superhero, but his thoughts are welded inexorably to the void. Too Much Coffee Man and his utterly useless comrades—Underwater Guy, Too Much Espresso Guy, and Too Much German White Chocolate Woman With Almonds—walk the wall for us even though it only looks like they're absentmindedly watching television.

Too Much Coffee Man is so tired but cannot sleep; he must stay as we would support our own. Because they are.

About the artist: The creator of Too Much Coffee Man is not the man of mystery that you would have hoped. He does not speak in oblique pithy verse. He does not live in mansioned solitude overlooking a distant, sparkling metropolis. He does not go from port to port under the cover of night, sending panels to nervous and furious editors who anxiously pace office floors long after closing time awaiting his next artistic spasm. Don't we wish. No, friends, he's Shannon Wheeler, a slave to the grind, be it the bean or the common working stone against which so many of us throw ourselves daily. When friends were asked to talk about him for this short bio, they all demanded anonymity. Many of them used the term "long suffering" to describe the relationship. When I phoned the artist to ask what he wanted said on his behalf, he replied, "Something about me being lashed to the mast of a ship in a raging sea of creative impulse, that the roiling forces of genius that constantly course through my . . ." That's when I hung up and got sick of this job. Enjoy the work, but don't try to understand Mr. Wheeler. Thankfully, that's his job.

Henry Rollins

TMCM vs. TM©M

TM©1993 SHANNON WHEELER

TMCM VS. TM©M

TOO MUCH COFFEE MAN
VS.
TRADEMARK COPYRIGHT MAN

QUESTION:
WHAT HAPPENS WHEN THE **UNSTOPPABLE** ENCOUNTERS THE **IMMOVABLE**?

ANSWER:
A **CONFLICT** OF SUCH SEVERITY, BY THE END ONLY **ONE** SHALL REMAIN TO TELL THE TALE...

IN ORDER TO GRASP THE **SCOPE** OF THIS COSMIC COLLISION, WE MUST TRAVEL BACK IN TIME...

TM©1993

TOO MUCH COFFEE MAN SITS DRINKING HIS MORNING CUP. WE NOW ENTER THE WORLD, NAY, THE UNIVERSE OF TMCM...

THIS SURE DOES MAKE ME FEEL GOOD!

AND, YOU KNOW, IF ONE CUP MAKES ME FEEL GOOD, THEN TWO CUPS WILL MAKE ME FEEL EVEN BETTER!

I FEEL KIND OF SICK AND UNSETTLED... PERHAPS IF I HAVE ANOTHER CUP I'LL BEGIN TO FEEL BETTER.

I'M NERVOUS, PARANOID, JITTERY, SICK TO MY STOMACH, AND TOTALLY INCAPABLE OF DOING ANYTHING PRODUCTIVE.
LOOKS LIKE IT'S TIME FOR...

THE TOILET!

TIME TO SIT AND CONTEMPLATE **LIFE**.

AS I SIT AND CONTEMPLATE, I BEGIN TO REALIZE HOW SHORT OUR LIVES ACTUALLY ARE.

I NEED TO **DO** SOMETHING... BUT WHEN I'M INVOLVED WITH A PROJECT, I LOSE TRACK OF TIME. I TURN AROUND AND YEARS OF MY LIFE ARE SUDDENLY **GONE**.

IF...I SIT AND DO NOTHING...THEN... TIME SEEMS TO SLOW...TO A CRAWL...
BUT...I ACCOMPLISH NOTHING.

IF I COULD MANAGE TO DO SOMETHING **AND** NOTHING AT THE **SAME** TIME, IT'LL SEEM LIKE LIFE LASTS **FOREVER**.

BUT I'M WASTING TIME THINKING ABOUT WASTING TIME.

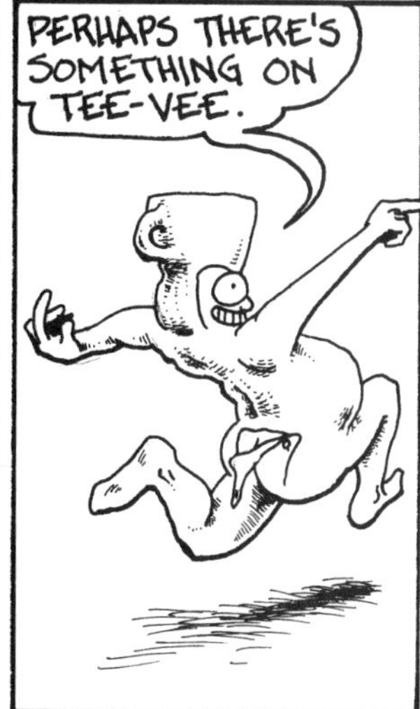
PERHAPS THERE'S SOMETHING ON TEE-VEE.

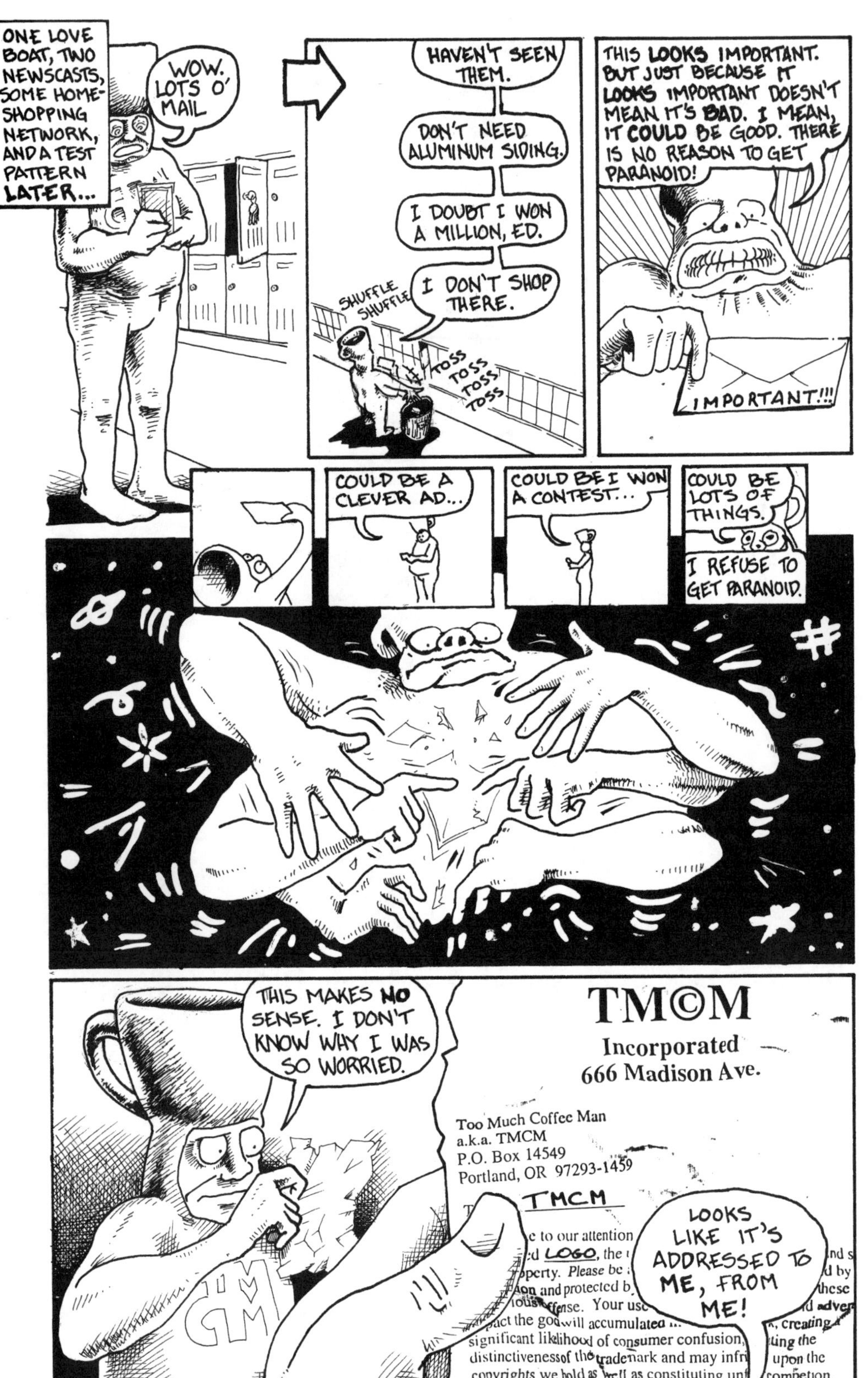

ONE LOVE BOAT, TWO NEWSCASTS, SOME HOME-SHOPPING NETWORK, AND A TEST PATTERN **LATER...**
WOW. LOTS O' MAIL
HAVEN'T SEEN THEM.
DON'T NEED ALUMINUM SIDING.
I DOUBT I WON A MILLION, ED.
I DON'T SHOP THERE.
SHUFFLE SHUFFLE
TOSS TOSS TOSS TOSS
THIS **LOOKS** IMPORTANT. BUT JUST BECAUSE IT **LOOKS** IMPORTANT DOESN'T MEAN IT'S **BAD**. I MEAN, IT **COULD** BE GOOD. THERE IS NO REASON TO GET PARANOID!
IMPORTANT!!!
COULD BE A CLEVER AD...
COULD BE I WON A CONTEST...
COULD BE LOTS OF THINGS.
I REFUSE TO GET PARANOID.
THIS MAKES **NO** SENSE. I DON'T KNOW WHY I WAS SO WORRIED.
TM©M
Incorporated
666 Madison Ave.
Too Much Coffee Man
a.k.a. TMCM
P.O. Box 14549
Portland, OR 97293-1459
TMCM
LOOKS LIKE IT'S ADDRESSED TO **ME**, FROM **ME**!

I HAVE NO IDEA WHAT THIS LETTER MEANS.

LIKE ANYONE WITH **TOO MUCH** FREE TIME, TMCM BUSES TO THE ADDRESS ON THE ENVELOPE.

THIS LOOKS LIKE THE PLACE.
TMCM

DO THEY **PICK** BAD ART TO GO IN CORPORATE OFFICES, OR DOES THE CORPORATE OFFICE **MAKE** THE ART LOOK **BAD**?

TMCM? HE'S **EXPECTING** YOU. GO RIGHT ON IN.
THIS IS A "**HEALTHY**" BUILDING–NO SMOKING IS ALLOWED.

"**NO SMOKING IS ALLOWED**"! WELL, THAT'S **GOOD**. PEOPLE SHOULDN'T **HAVE** TO SMOKE IF THEY DON'T **WANT** TO.
TMCM

WHEN **TMCM** MEETS **TMCM**, IS THERE VIOLENCE? YES. THE VIOLENCE OF THE **LEGAL WORLD**.
COME IN. I'VE BEEN **EXPECTING** YOU.

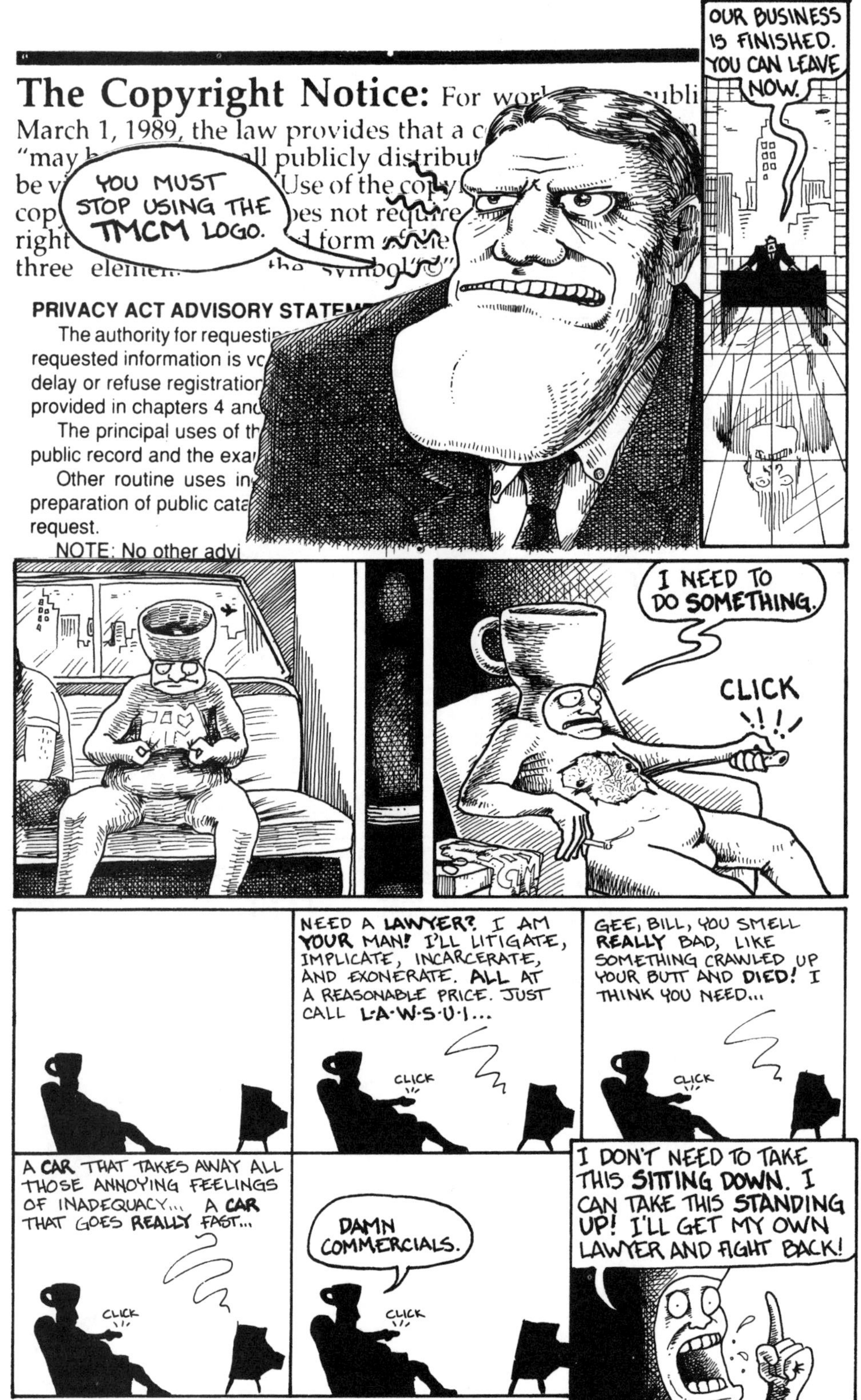
The Copyright Notice:
YOU MUST STOP USING THE TMCM LOGO.
PRIVACY ACT ADVISORY STATEMENT
OUR BUSINESS IS FINISHED. YOU CAN LEAVE NOW.
I NEED TO DO SOMETHING.
CLICK
NEED A LAWYER? I AM YOUR MAN! I'LL LITIGATE, IMPLICATE, INCARCERATE, AND EXONERATE. ALL AT A REASONABLE PRICE. JUST CALL L·A·W·S·U·I...
CLICK
GEE, BILL, YOU SMELL REALLY BAD, LIKE SOMETHING CRAWLED UP YOUR BUTT AND DIED! I THINK YOU NEED...
CLICK
A CAR THAT TAKES AWAY ALL THOSE ANNOYING FEELINGS OF INADEQUACY... A CAR THAT GOES REALLY FAST...
CLICK
DAMN COMMERCIALS.
CLICK
I DON'T NEED TO TAKE THIS SITTING DOWN. I CAN TAKE THIS STANDING UP! I'LL GET MY OWN LAWYER AND FIGHT BACK!

YOU HAVE **NOTHING** TO **WORRY** ABOUT– I'VE BEEN COLLECTING **PAPERWORK** ON THIS CASE

AND WE HAVE A **PRECEDENT.**

ABSOLUTELY NOTHING TO WORRY ABOUT. IN FACT YOU DIDN'T EVEN NEED TO COME HERE TODAY. MY RETAINER FEE COVERS...

IT'S WORSE THAN I THOUGHT!

IT **IS** WORSE THAN **TMCM** THINKS. EVEN THOUGH OUR HERO NOW HAS A LAWYER, TM©M HAS A CUP ON HIS HEAD. AND NOW THEY FACE OFF... **CUP** AGAINST **CUP**, **MUG** AGAINST **MUG.**

I'VE FILED A **TRADEMARK** ON THE "CUP-ON-THE-HEAD" AND **COPYRIGHTS** ON MANIC BEHAVIOR, PARANOIA, COFFEE ADDICTION, AND EXAGGERATED EXPRESSIONS.

BURP
YOU ATE MY LAWYER.
HEE
HA HA HA
HA HA HA
HAWHAW HAWHAW
HA HA HA HA
YOU ATE MY LAWYER!
WACK

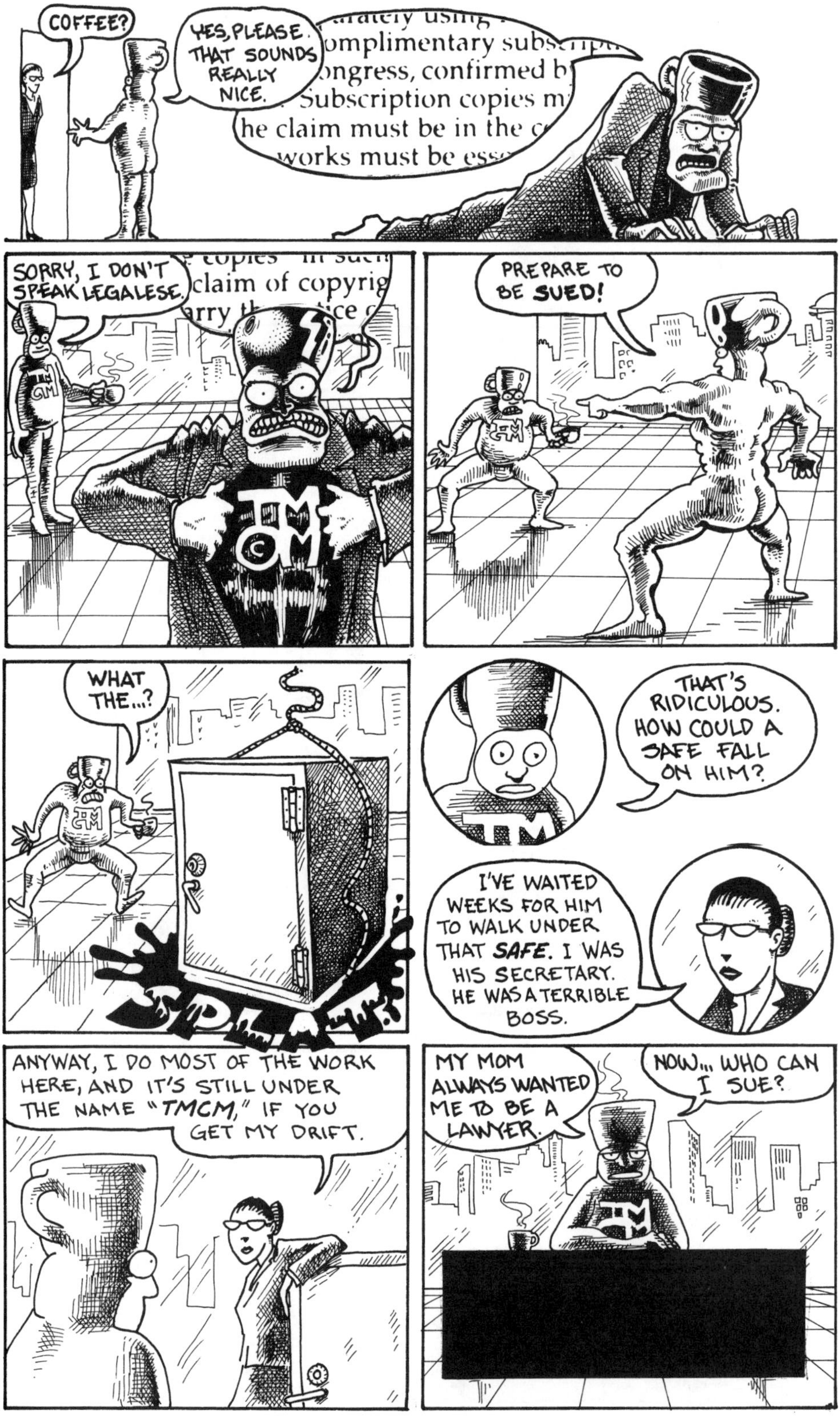

COFFEE?
YES, PLEASE. THAT SOUNDS REALLY NICE.
omplimentary subs
ongress, confirmed b
Subscription copies m
he claim must be in the c
works must be ess
SORRY, I DON'T SPEAK LEGALESE.
claim of copyrig
PREPARE TO BE **SUED**!
WHAT THE...?
THAT'S RIDICULOUS. HOW COULD A SAFE FALL ON HIM?

TMCM vs. TM©M
OPEN 24 HRS
FAX
FAX
CHUGGA
CHUGGA
CHUGGA
CHUGGA
CHUGGA
PLEASE COUNT YOUR COPIES

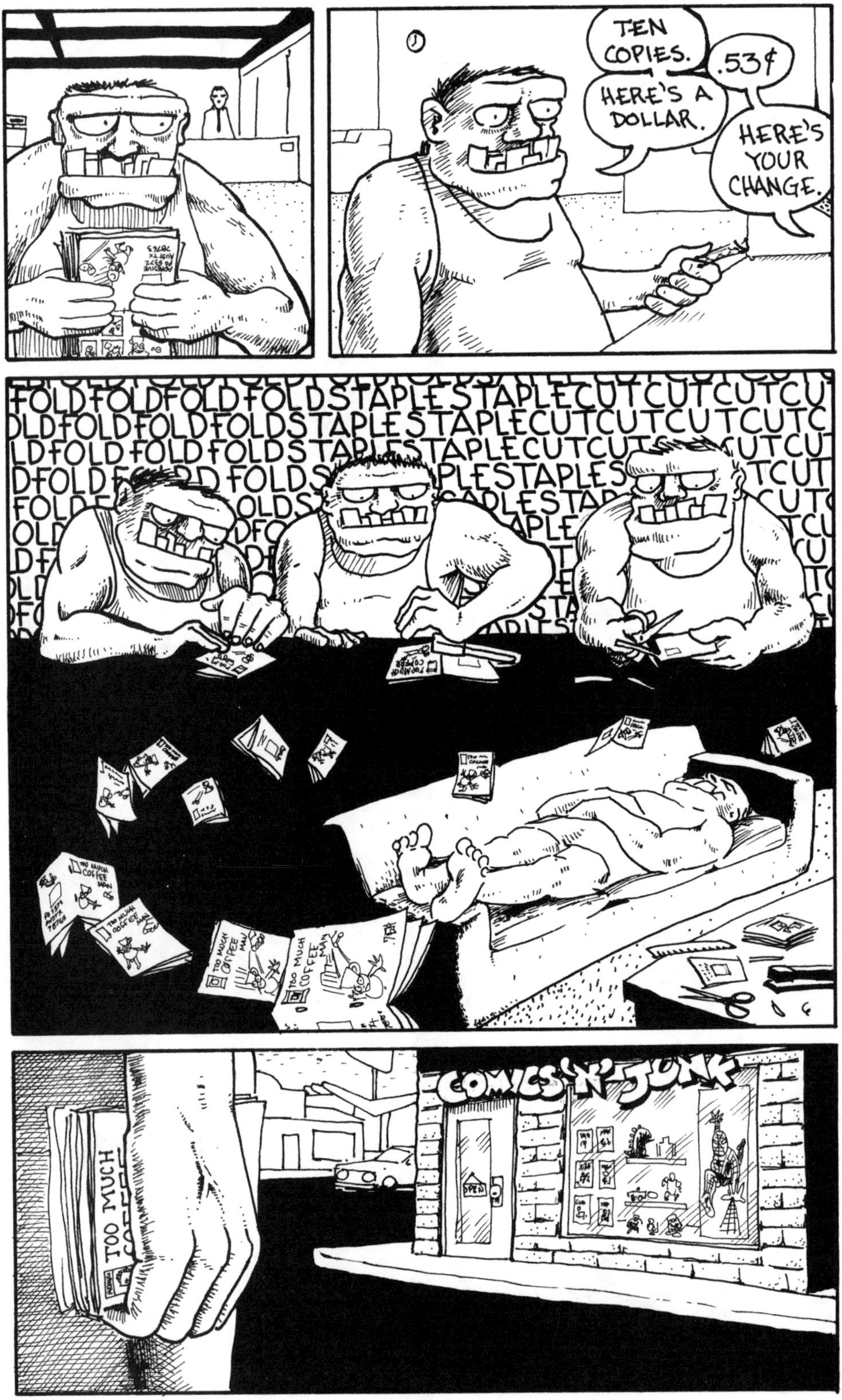

TEN COPIES.
HERE'S A DOLLAR.
.53¢
HERE'S YOUR CHANGE.

COMICS 'N' JUNK
OPEN
TOO MUCH

I WANT THAT COMIC WITH GOLD FOIL, HOLOGRAM, DIE-CUT, AND POLY-BAGGED. BUT I CAN'T **REMEMBER** WHAT ITS **NAME** IS.
WE'RE SOLD OUT.

DO YOU HAVE THE COMIC WITH THE **BULLET HOLE**?
FROM MALIBU?
NO, I MEAN THE **REAL** BULLET HOLE.

HOW ARE MY **MINI-COMICS** SELLING?
GOOD. GOOD. PEOPLE LIKE 'EM.

LOTS OF PEOPLE PICK 'EM UP, READ 'EM, AND BUST A GUT LAUGHING BEFORE THEY PUT 'EM BACK.

I MADE SOME MORE IF YOU WANT THEM.

THEY'RE SELLING PRETTY GOOD. WHY DON'T YOU GIVE ME **FIVE** MORE?

DO YOU WANT THAT IN **CASH** OR **TRADE CREDIT**?
CASH.

.81¢
THANKS.

I WISH I WAS **MORE** POPULAR.

YOU'RE GOOD. YOU JUST NEED **EXPOSURE**.

HAVE YOU TRIED DOING A CARTOON FOR THE LOCAL LIBERAL RAG? IF YOU HAD SOMETHING IN **THERE**, YOU'D BE MORE **POPULAR** THAN YOU COULD STAND.

AND IT WOULD HELP **SELL** YOUR MINI-COMIC.

ESPECIALLY IF YOU MENTION **WHERE** TO BUY THEM.

COMICS'N'JUNK

I TRIED THAT ONCE. THE **ART DIRECTOR** WOULDN'T EVEN RETURN MY PHONE CALLS.

MY WIFE HAD AN **AFFAIR** WITH THE **PUBLISHER**. IT'S OVER NOW, BUT HE OWES ME A FAVOR. BESIDES, I ADVERTISE IN HIS PAPER.

I'M SURE I COULD GET YOU IN.

BUT BEWARE. IT'S LIKE SPOCK SAYS: *"SOMETIMES WANTING SOMETHING IS BETTER THAN HAVING IT. IT'S NOT LOGICAL BUT IT'S TRUE!"*

DON'T QUOTE STAR TREK AT ME.

Coffee
SHANNON WHEELER
WHAT A COP-OUT ENDING.
HEY!
JOEL? WHAT ARE YOU DOING HERE AT TWO IN THE MORNING?
TRIXIE?!

IT'S BEEN ONE SCREWY NIGHT. IS IT A FULL MOON OR WHAT? HOW'RE TRICKS WITH YOU?
OKAY, I GUESS.
TRIXIE, I HAVEN'T SEEN YOU FOR A WHILE. ARE YOU STILL GOING TO SCHOOL AND WORKING?
YOU BET.
SO, HOW ARE THINGS?
WORK SUCKS, SCHOOL SUCKS, MY HOUSING SCENE SUCKS, MY CAR IS BREAKING DOWN, I THINK I HAVE A LUMP, AND I'M OUT OF CIGARETTES... THE ONLY THING THAT IS GOOD IS MY ROMANTIC LIFE.
REALLY?
NO, ROMANCE SUCKS TOO.
I'VE DECIDED THAT LIFE IS TOO SHORT TO BE GOOD.
THAT WAS MY COFFEE.
REMEMBER WHEN WE WERE YOUNG: WE LOOKED FORWARD TO THINGS. I CAN'T WAIT TO DRIVE. I CAN'T WAIT TO GET A BOYFRIEND. I CAN'T WAIT TO GRADUATE HIGHSCHOOL. ETC. ETC.
NOW IT'S REMEMBER HOW GREAT HIGHSCHOOL WAS. OR NOTHING COMPARES TO THE FEELING OF FIRST LOVE. LIFE WAS SO MUCH BETTER BACK WHEN WE WERE YOUNG.
SOMEWHERE BETWEEN ANTICIPATION AND NOSTALGIA WE SHOULD HAVE BEEN HAPPY.

HOW'S IT GOING WITH WHAT'S-HER-NAME?
YOU KNOW HER NAME IS EVE, AND WE'RE BREAKING UP.
WHAT?
BUT YOU TWO HAVE BEEN GOING OUT FOREVER! I THOUGHT YOU WERE GOING TO MARRY HER.
I'M JUST NOT IN LOVE ANYMORE. WE'VE GONE OUT SINCE HIGH SCHOOL, I WANT TO SEE WHAT ELSE IS OUT THERE.
HOW'S SHE TAKING THIS?
I HAVEN'T TOLD HER YET.
IT'S JUST TOO HARD. I CAN'T STAND TO BREAK HER HEART, BUT I CAN'T DEAL WITH GOING OUT WITH HER ANYMORE. I'M AT A LOSS.
I KNOW WHAT TO DO.
WHAT?
BE SUCH A JERK THAT SHE LEAVES YOU... YOU'LL BOTH END UP WINNERS.
IT WOULDN'T WORK. SHE'S IN LOVE WITH ME. ABUSE JUST INTENSIFIES LOVE.
THEN DO HER THE FAVOR AND CUT IT OFF COLD TURKEY OR ELSE IT WILL DRAG ON UNTIL YOU HATE EACH OTHER.

BUT REALLY
YOU SHOULD STAY WITH HER. IF SHE'S IN LOVE WITH YOU, THEN YOU'RE IN THE KING'S CHAIR.
IF SOMEONE'S IN LOVE THEY'LL DO ANYTHING TO MAKE YOU HAPPY. THEY'LL HAVE SEX WHERE YOU WANT, HOW YOU WANT, AND WHEN YOU WANT.
THEY'LL GIVE YOU BACK RUBS, COOK FOOD, DO HOUSEWORK-- IT'S GREAT!
IT'S THE IDEAL SITUATION!
IT'S NOT IDEAL. IT SUCKS! SHE GOES THROUGH MY STUFF. SHE RESENTS IT WHEN I WANT TO BE ALONE, AND SHE'S INSANELY JEALOUS OF ANY FEMALE FRIEND OF MINE. I'M GOING CRAZY.
I GUESS IT'S ONE OF THOSE THINGS THAT SUCKS BUT YOU CAN'T COMPLAIN ABOUT.
YOU CAN'T COMPLAIN ABOUT BEING WHITE.
OR BEING MALE.
OR HAVING TOO MUCH FREE TIME.
TOO MANY FRIENDS.
TOO MUCH MONEY.
HEY! LAST NIGHT I REALIZED THAT EVERY-ONE ON THIS PLANET IS GOING TO BE DEAD IN 200 YEARS.
I DON'T GET IT.
OLD AGE.

I'M SUCH A **WIMP.**

I CAN'T BELIEVE I'VE LET THIS RELATIONSHIP DRAG ON FOR AS **LONG** AS I HAVE. IT'S MAKING ME **MISERABLE.**

I'VE GOT TO BE A **MAN** AND JUST **BREAK** IT OFF. IF SHE **CRIES,** SHE **CRIES.** I CAN'T LET THAT SWAY ME.

I **KNOW** THAT BREAKING UP WITH HER IS THE **RIGHT** THING TO DO. THIS DYSFUNCTIONAL RELATIONSHIP HAS **DRAGGED ON** WAY **TOO LONG!**

OH, **JEEZ**. HI, EVE. I DIDN'T EXPECT YOU...

...BUT I'M KIND OF GLAD YOU'RE HERE. I **NEED** TO TALK TO YOU.

YOU WANT TO **BREAK UP**, DON'T YOU?

WHAT?!! NO, OF COURSE NOT... I JUST THINK WE SHOULD, YOU KNOW, **TALK**...

I'M NOT SICK OF YOU... I REALLY CARE ABOUT YOU.

IT'S NOT THAT I WANT TO BREAK UP...
I JUST NEED MORE SPACE.

I'M GOING THROUGH SOME CHANGES, AND I NEED TO THINK THROUGH SOME THINGS.

I JUST CAN'T DEAL WITH THIS INTENSE OF A RELATIONSHIP.

YOU'RE SMART AND BEAUTIFUL- IF I WAS GOING TO GO OUT WITH ANYONE, IT WOULD BE YOU.

IT'S BETTER FOR BOTH OF US THIS WAY.

I VALUE YOU, AS A PERSON... I WANT TO STAY FRIENDS.

I REALLY CARE ABOUT YOU.

DON'T BE HURT.
PLEASE.

THIS HAS TO STOP.

ARE YOU OKAY?
THIS IS A MESS. I'VE GOT TO GO HOME.
HE'S BREAKING UP WITH ME.
I HATE BREAKING UP WITH HER, BUT I'M SURE IT'S FOR THE BEST.
NOT WITH A BANG BUT WITH A DUD.

MY ROOMMATES ARE SUCH SLOBS.

WHAT A MISERABLE SET OF CIRCUMSTANCES.

ARE YOU AWAKE?
YEAH.

CLICK
I THINK HE'S GOING TO BREAK UP WITH ME.
FINALLY.
TO BE CONTINUED...

SHANNON WHEELER 1994©

POP
SNAP
SUPER
SUGER
CUBE
NOW WITHOUT THE CEREAL
INGREDIEN
SUGAR
MILK
MILK

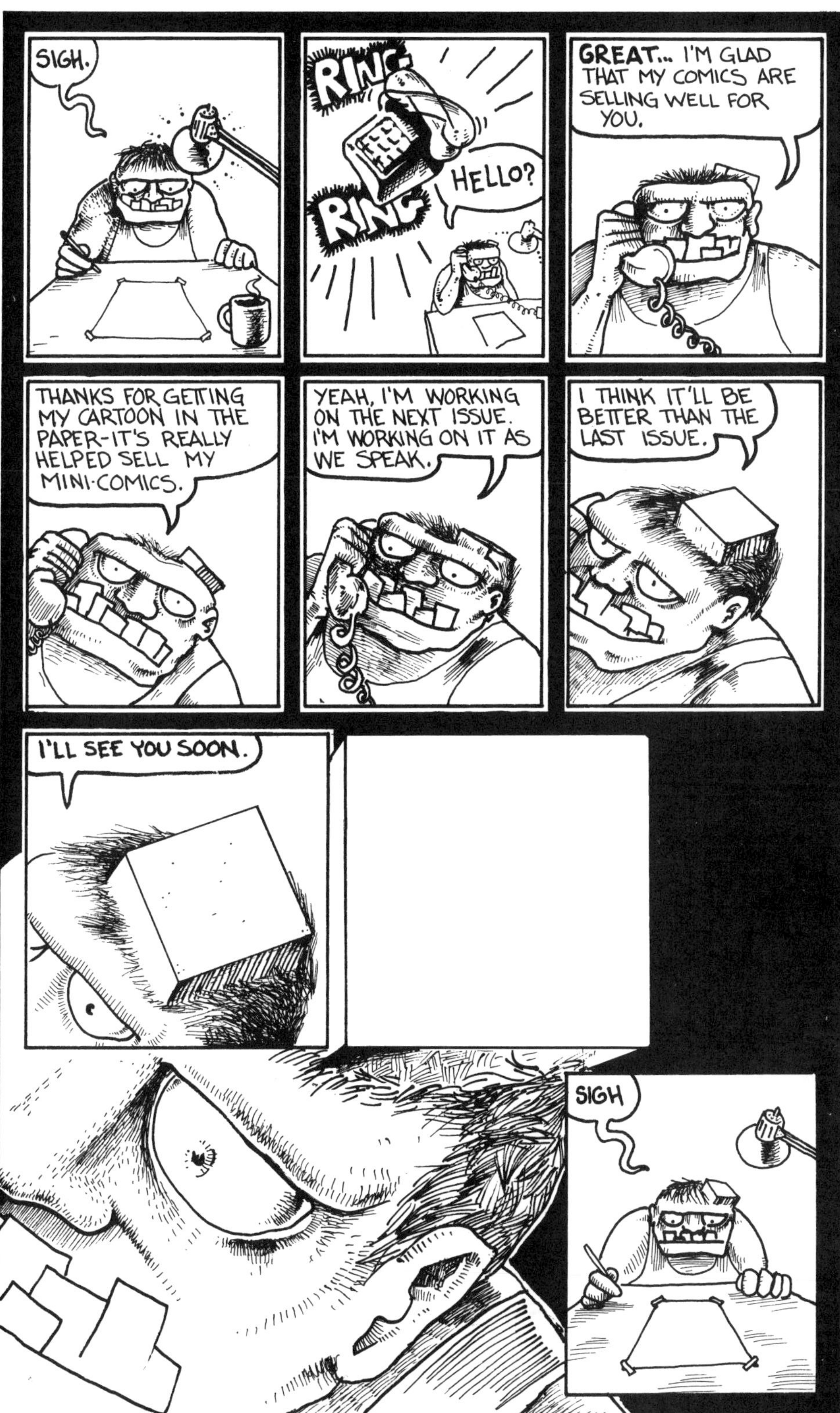
SIGH.
RING
RING
HELLO?
GREAT... I'M GLAD THAT MY COMICS ARE SELLING WELL FOR YOU.
THANKS FOR GETTING MY CARTOON IN THE PAPER-IT'S REALLY HELPED SELL MY MINI-COMICS.
YEAH, I'M WORKING ON THE NEXT ISSUE. I'M WORKING ON IT AS WE SPEAK.
I THINK IT'LL BE BETTER THAN THE LAST ISSUE.
I'LL SEE YOU SOON.
SIGH

FOLD FOLD FOLD FOLD STAPLE
STAPLES

CUT CUT CUT CUT CUT

I BROUGHT YOU SOME MORE MINI-COMICS.
I'LL WRITE YOU A CHECK.
I'M GONNA LOOK AROUND. ANYTHING NEW?
SAME OLD **CRAP** –JUST NEW **FLIES.**

SO MANY COMIC BOOKS.
WHY BOTHER MAKING ANOTHER ONE?
ANOTHER PEBBLE ON THE BEACH, ANOTHER DROP IN THE OCEAN. THERE'S NO POINT. NO HOPE.
TOO MUCH COFFEE MAN!!! I LOVE TOO MUCH COFFEE MAN!
I HAVE THIS ISSUE.
I'M GOING TO BUY ANOTHER ONE FOR MY COLLECTION.
WHEN DO YOU GET THE NEXT ISSUE?
SOON.
CAN YOU HOLD ONE FOR ME WHEN IT COMES IN?
SURE, KID.
TOO MUCH COFFEE MAN IS THE BEST!
I KNOW THE GIRL WHO DRAWS IT.
YOU DO NOT!
I'M GETTING MORE POPULAR, AREN'T I?
YEP. THE NEWSPAPER HAS REALLY HELPED YOUR POPULARITY.
JUST TELL ME WHEN I'M POPULAR ENOUGH TO BE A SNOB.
NOT YET.
YOU KNOW, IT'S PRETTY WEIRD THAT YOU STAND THERE AND WATCH PEOPLE READ YOUR COMIC.
WEIRD LIKE AN IRONIC KIND OF WEIRD?
NO... WEIRD LIKE A MASTURBATORY SORT OF WEIRD.
OH.

SCOOT
HEY, HOW'RE YOU DOING? IT'S ME...YOUR CARTOONIST.
TERRIBLE. I HAVE WRITER'S BLOCK, AND I DON'T KNOW WHAT TO DO ABOUT IT.
SURE, I'VE TRIED TAKING A BREAK, BUT IT'S NO GOOD. I HAVE PERFORMANCE ANXIETY. IT WAS A LOT EASIER TO DRAW CARTOONS WHEN NO ONE READ MY STUFF.
YOU HAVE AN IDEA? GREAT, MAYBE I CAN USE IT. WHAT IS IT?
I CAN'T USE THAT. IT'S STUPID-EVERYONE HAS DONE A CARTOON ABOUT TRYING TO COME UP WITH A CARTOON. IT'S AN OLD IDEA-TOTALLY CLICHÉ.

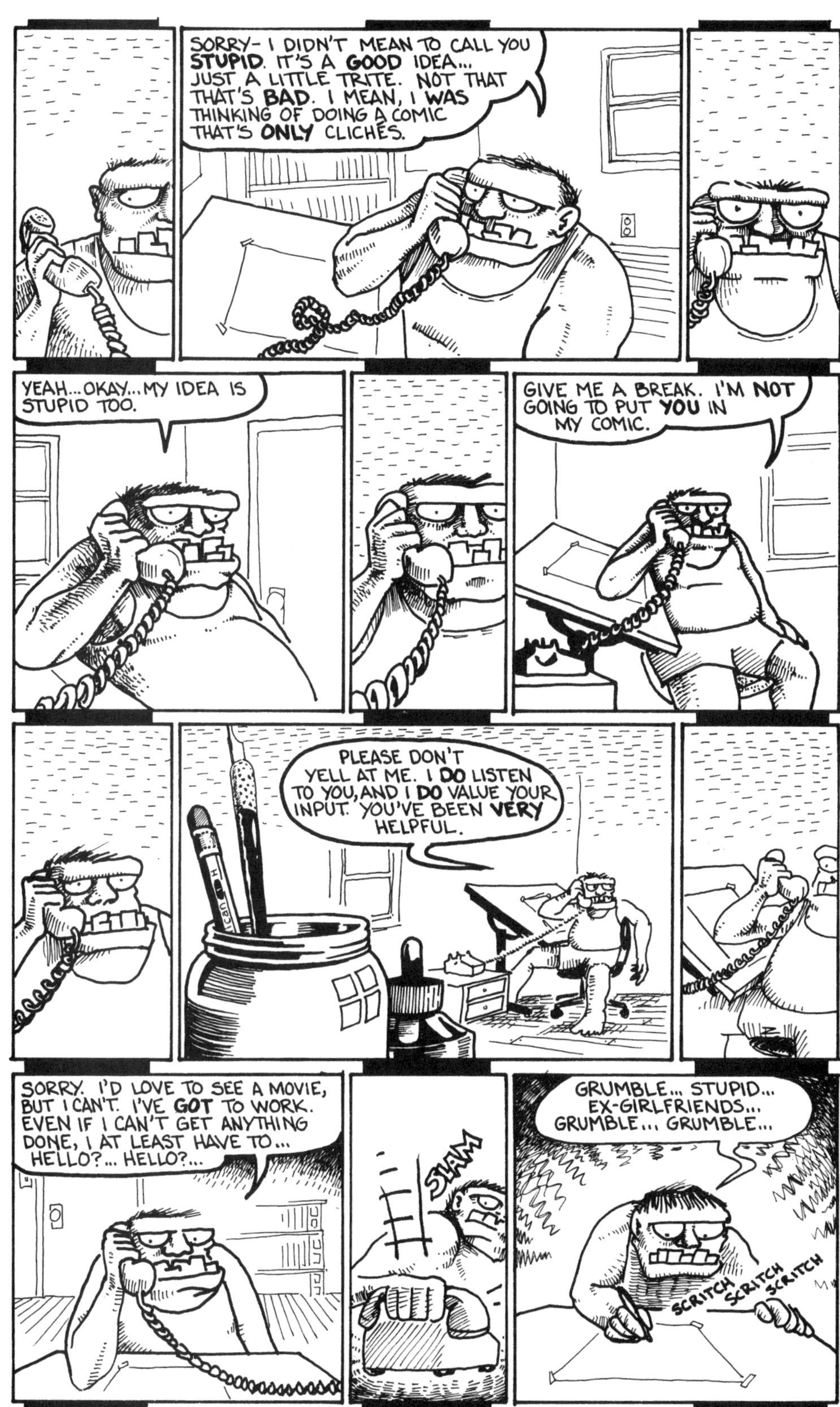
SORRY- I DIDN'T MEAN TO CALL YOU **STUPID**. IT'S A **GOOD** IDEA... JUST A LITTLE TRITE. NOT THAT THAT'S **BAD**. I MEAN, I **WAS** THINKING OF DOING A COMIC THAT'S **ONLY** CLICHÉS.
YEAH...OKAY...MY IDEA IS STUPID TOO.
GIVE ME A BREAK. I'M **NOT** GOING TO PUT **YOU** IN MY COMIC.
PLEASE DON'T YELL AT ME. I **DO** LISTEN TO YOU, AND I **DO** VALUE YOUR INPUT. YOU'VE BEEN **VERY** HELPFUL.
SORRY. I'D LOVE TO SEE A MOVIE, BUT I CAN'T. I'VE **GOT** TO WORK. EVEN IF I CAN'T GET ANYTHING DONE, I AT LEAST HAVE TO... HELLO?... HELLO?...
SLAM
GRUMBLE... STUPID... EX-GIRLFRIENDS... GRUMBLE... GRUMBLE...
SCRITCH SCRITCH SCRITCH

©SHANNON WHEELER
VENICE
ADVOCATE
FINE PRINT
POCHO
SHANNON'S WORLD

ENTER: CLICHÉ

I SELFLESSLY FIGHT CRIME WITH MY MIGHTY POWER.

I AM A SUPER-HERO!

I AM CLICHÉ!

AAAAAAAAAAAAAAAAAAAAAAAAAAAAAAAAAAAAAAAA
OUT OF COFFEE.

WHEN THE GOING GETS TOUGH, THE TOUGH GET GOING.

ANOTHER DAY, ANOTHER DOLLAR.

"X" MARKS THE SPOT.
CAFÉ-X
CAFÉ-X

UH-OH.
Sorry we're CLOSED

HE'S GONE... OVER THE EDGE... I'VE GOT TO STOP HIM BEFORE SOME-ONE GETS HURT.
SO NEAR AND YET SO FAR! THIS IS THE LAST STRAW! I CAN'T TAKE IT ANYMORE!
BANG
BANG
BANG

THERE'S A **TIME** AND A **PLACE** FOR **EVERYTHING**...

BUT YOU'VE BEEN **CAUGHT** WITH YOUR HAND IN THE **COOKIE JAR!!!** WELL, **WHAT** DO YOU HAVE TO SAY FOR YOURSELF?

I GUESS **THAT'S** THE WAY THE **COOKIE CRUMBLES**.

IT'S LIKE I **ALWAYS** SAY, IF YOU WANT TO HEAR THE **MUSIC**, YOU'VE GOT TO PAY THE **PIPER**.

THE WEED OF **CRIME** BEARS A **BITTER** FRUIT.

IT'S BETTER TO **DIE** ON YOUR **FEET** THAN TO **LIVE** ON YOUR **KNEES**.

THE **COWARD** DIES A **THOUSAND DEATHS**, BUT THE **HERO** ONLY **ONE**.

THEN AGAIN, HE WHO FIGHTS AND **RUNS AWAY** LIVES TO FIGHT **ANOTHER DAY**!

RAT-A TAT-A TAT A TAT

STOP! OR I'LL **SHOOT**!

DAMN, I'M SPILLING MY **COFFEE**.

SHOOT POW ZING POP ZIP

HEY, GUNS DON'T KILL PEOPLE, **PEOPLE** KILL **PEOPLE**.

C'MON AND **FIGHT LIKE A MAN**. LET'S SETTLE THIS **BAREHANDED, MANO A MANO**. OR ARE YOU **SCARED**?

POW

I'M GONNA HIT YOU SO HARD, I'M GONNA KNOCK YOU INTO THE MIDDLE OF **NEXT WEEK.**

ANOTHER JOB WELL DONE.

GOT TO SET YOUR SIGHTS HIGH.

AND SHOOT FOR THE STARS.

I WILL **NOT** REST UNTIL THE STREETS ARE SAFE AGAIN, JUSTICE IS SERVED, AND MY UNCLE'S DEATH IS AVENGED.

I SENSE **MORE** CRIME. WILL THEY EVER LEARN?

CRIME DOESN'T PAY!

NOW **THAT'S** PUTTING YOUR HEADS TOGETHER.

HOME IS WHERE THE HEART IS, WHERE THE CHICKENS COME HOME TO ROOST. AND A MAN'S HOME IS HIS CASTLE.

SCREEE

MUCH LATER.

KNOCK KNOCK

OPPORTUNITY?

WHAT

SURPRISED?! IT'S THE "MIDDLE OF NEXT WEEK"! IS THIS A CASE OF OUT OF SIGHT... OUT OF MIND?

YOU'RE WRONG. ABSENCE MAKES THE HEART GROW FONDER.

I'VE BEEN WAITING FOR THIS DAY.

GOOD THINGS COME TO THOSE WHO WAIT.

HE WHO HESITATES IS LOST.

HASTE MAKES WASTE!

YOU'VE GOT TO STRIKE WHILE THE IRON IS HOT.

OUT OF THE FRYING PAN AND INTO THE FIRE.

IF YOU CAN'T STAND THE HEAT, GET OUT OF THE KITCHEN.

DON'T COUNT YOUR CHICKENS UNTIL ALL YOUR EGGS HAVE HATCHED.

DON'T PUT ALL YOUR EGGS IN ONE BASKET.

ONE BIRD IN YOUR HAND IS WORTH TWO IN THE BUSH.

ONE HAND WASHES THE OTHER.

YOU'VE GOT YOUR HANDS FULL.

THIS HAS GOTTEN OUT OF HAND.

THEN I MUST HAND IT TO YOU.

YOU CAN'T HAVE YOUR CAKE AND EAT IT TOO.

ONE MAN'S FOOD IS ANOTHER'S POISON.

THE GOOD MUST SUFFER WITH THE BAD.

UM...UH...

UH...

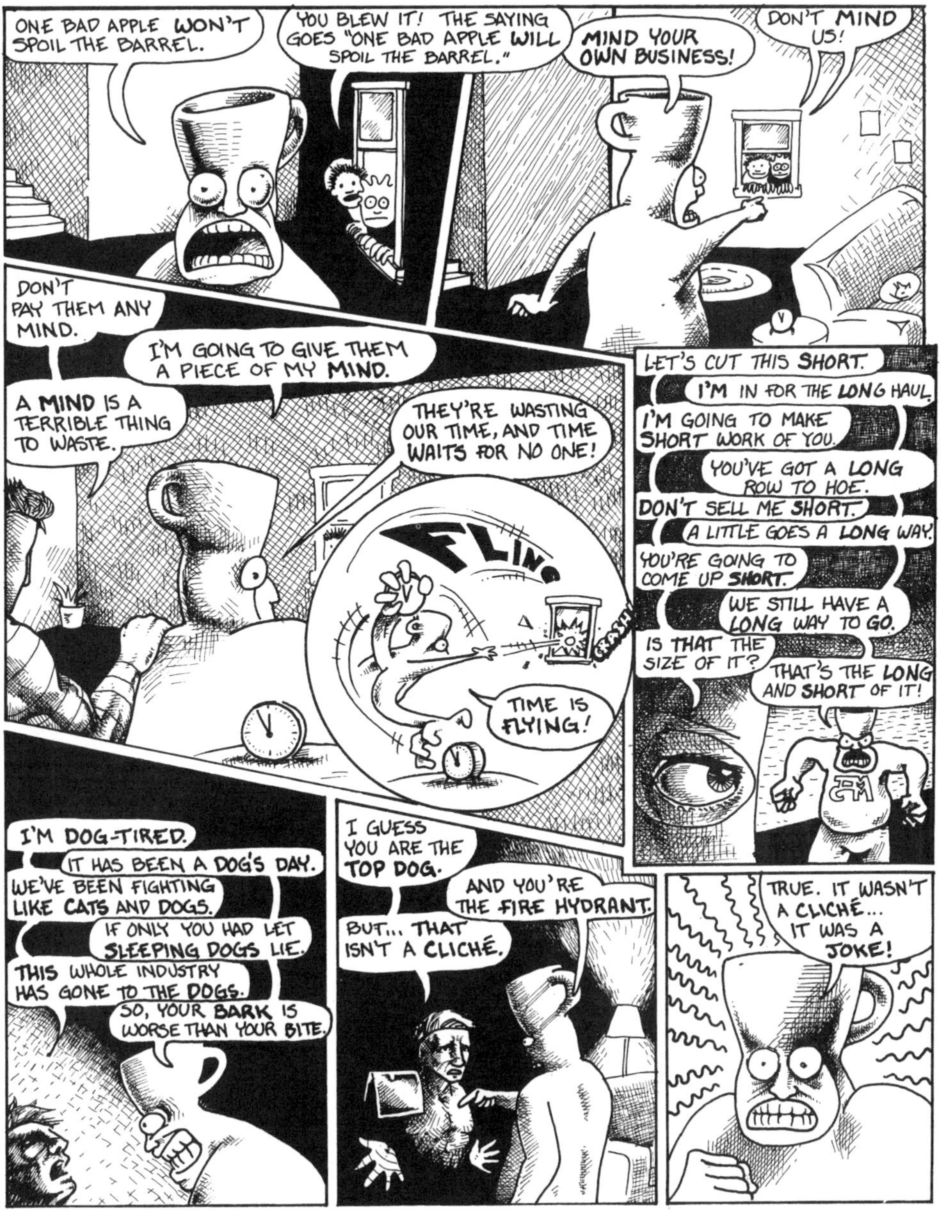

ONE BAD APPLE **WON'T** SPOIL THE BARREL.

YOU BLEW IT! THE SAYING GOES "ONE BAD APPLE **WILL** SPOIL THE BARREL."

MIND YOUR OWN BUSINESS!

DON'T **MIND** US!

DON'T PAY THEM ANY MIND.

I'M GOING TO GIVE THEM A PIECE OF MY **MIND.**

A **MIND** IS A TERRIBLE THING TO WASTE.

THEY'RE WASTING OUR TIME, AND TIME WAITS FOR NO ONE!

FLING

CRASH!

TIME IS FLYING!

LET'S CUT THIS **SHORT.**

I'M IN FOR THE **LONG** HAUL.

I'M GOING TO MAKE SHORT WORK OF YOU.

YOU'VE GOT A **LONG** ROW TO HOE.

DON'T SELL ME **SHORT.**

A LITTLE GOES A **LONG** WAY.

YOU'RE GOING TO COME UP **SHORT.**

WE STILL HAVE A **LONG** WAY TO **GO.**

IS **THAT** THE SIZE OF IT?

THAT'S THE **LONG** AND **SHORT** OF IT!

I'M **DOG-TIRED.**

IT HAS BEEN A **DOG'S DAY.**

WE'VE BEEN FIGHTING LIKE **CATS AND DOGS.**

IF ONLY YOU HAD LET **SLEEPING DOGS** LIE.

THIS WHOLE INDUSTRY HAS GONE TO THE **DOGS.**

SO, YOUR **BARK** IS WORSE THAN YOUR **BITE.**

I GUESS YOU ARE THE **TOP DOG.**

AND YOU'RE THE **FIRE HYDRANT.**

BUT... **THAT** ISN'T A **CLICHÉ.**

TRUE. IT WASN'T A **CLICHÉ**... IT WAS A **JOKE!**

AND HERE'S THE PUNCH LINE!

POW

I GIVE UP... YOU'RE A BIGGER CLICHÉ THAN **I AM**...

I NEED SOME COFFEE.

IN RETROSPECT I SEE HOW **FOOLISH** IT WAS FOR CLICHÉ TO PUT **ALL** HIS **FAITH** AND **POWER** IN THESE **TRITE** SAYINGS.

AFTER ALL, IT'S A FINE LINE BETWEEN SAYINGS THAT MAKE SENSE.

END

VARIETY
THE RELATIONSHIP
THE RELATIONSHIP
I HOPE THIS IS GOOD.

THE REVIEWERS LIKED IT.
THE REVIEWERS DIDN'T HAVE TO PAY SIX BUCKS TO SEE IT.

I **HATE** THE PREVIEWS. THEY TELL YOU THE ENTIRE PLOT.
THE PREVIEWS ARE THE **BEST** PART.

IF YOU SEE THE PREVIEWS AND READ A COUPLE REVIEWS, YOU CAN SKIP THE MOVIE ENTIRELY AND STILL TALK ABOUT IT AS THOUGH YOU'VE SEEN IT.

NOBODY WANTS TO **REALLY** TALK ABOUT THINGS ANYWAY— THEY JUST WANT A MUTUAL AFFIRMATION OF SHARED ACTIVITY.
I GUESS PEOPLE FEEL LESS ALONE IN THE UNIVERSE IF THEY THINK OTHER PEOPLE ARE DOING THE SAME THING THEY'RE DOING.

LOVE IS THE **BEST** THING IN THE WORLD FOR CREATING THE TEMPORARY ILLUSION THAT YOU'RE NOT ALONE IN THE UNIVERSE.

I **LOVE** FALLING IN LOVE. UNFORTUNATELY I TEND NOT TO **LIKE** THE PEOPLE I FALL IN LOVE WITH.
THAT **IS** A PROBLEM.

HOW COME **WE** NEVER WENT OUT?
BECAUSE I DON'T **NOT** LIKE YOU ENOUGH. BESIDES, YOU'RE A **WIMP**.

HOW DO-
SHHH- WE'LL MISS THE PREVIEWS.
YOU'RE RIGHT ABOUT THE PREVIEWS.

THAT SURE DID SUCK.
THE RELAT
"WONDERFUL"
"GREAT"
"THE BEST"
NOW SHOWING

WHAT DO YOU EXPECT WITH REVIEWS THAT ARE ALL ONE-WORD QUIPS: "WONDERFUL"..."TERRIFIC"... "SPLENDID"...

YOU KNOW THEY DID A LOT OF EDITING TO GET THOSE "GLOWING" REVIEWS.
SOMETIMES I HATE MOVIES.

IF I WERE A VILLAIN AND HAD THE HERO, I WOULDN'T FOLLOW THE RULE AND TALK OR GLOAT. I'D JUST KILL HIM. AND I WOULDN'T DO IT IN SOME WEIRD OR FANCY WAY. I'D JUST SHOOT HIM IN THE HEAD QUICK 'N' EASY.

WHENEVER A KILLER IS KILLED, EVERYONE RELAXES... THEN SUDDENLY -BAM- HE'S BACK ON THE SET, EVERYONE IS SHOCKED, THEY KILL HIM FOR GOOD, AND EVERYONE RELAXES AGAIN, AND THE MOVIE'S OVER.
THAT'S WHAT'S CALLED A FAUX-FINIS.
WHAT'S THAT?
THE FAKE FINISH.
DID YOU LEARN THAT IN YOUR FILM CLASS?
NO, I MADE IT UP.
BOOKS

FLIGHTPATH coff
5011
DUVAL

THERE ARE SO MANY THINGS THAT ARE THE SAME IN EVERY MOVIE BUT NEVER OCCUR IN REAL LIFE.

EVERY TIME PEOPLE GO TO A BAR, THERE'S A FIGHT. I'VE BEEN TO A MILLION BARS AND NEVER SEEN A FIGHT... MUCH LESS BEEN IN ONE
OFFICE
BEER N BOOZE BAR

WANT TO GET A BEER?
YOU BET.

I LOVE TO DRINK.

BEER: HOW PRETTY YOU ARE. SO GOLDEN AND READY TO DRINK. NOBLE LITTLE BUBBLES IN YOUR RACE TO JOIN THE FOAMY HEAD, YOU HELP ME TO FEEL SO GOOD. YOU NEVER LET ME DOWN. YOU ARE THE PERFECT FRIEND.

YOU KNOW, I HATE FRIENDS WHO'LL DISAPPEAR AS SOON AS THEY GET A GIRLFRIEND- THEN, WHEN THEY BREAK UP, THEY EXPECT THEIR FRIENDS TO BE ALL SYMPATHETIC AND SUPPORTIVE.

UH... SORRY.

HEY, YOU'RE ON MY JACKET.

SORRY, HERE YOU GO.

THANKS.

THAT WAS WEIRD.
WHEW

DRINK UP! WE'RE CLOSING!!!

JUST LIKE COCKROACHES- TURN ON THE LIGHTS AND THEY SCURRY AWAY.
EVERYTHING LOOKED SO NICE WHEN IT WAS DARK.

TIME TO TEACH YOU MY PHILOSOPHY OF LIFE: "NEVER, EVER, DRIVE WHEN YOU'RE DRUNK. BUT, IF YOU DO DRIVE DRUNK, BE SURE TO WEAR A SEAT BELT."
TOO BAD WE DON'T HAVE A CAR.
NUGS
BEER BOOZE BAR

IT'S A REALLY LONG WALK TO YOUR HOUSE. YOU CAN STAY AT MY PLACE. BUT ABSOLUTELY **NO** MONKEY BUSINESS!
WELL, HERE WE ARE IN ALL ITS GLORY.

YOU SURE YOU DON'T WANT TO **FOOL AROUND**? IT WOULDN'T HAVE TO **MEAN** ANYTHING.

HEY!!! YOU GET TO **SLEEP** ON THE **COUCH!** OKAY? GUYS ARE SUCH **MORONS!**
SHOVE
OOF... SORRY.

I SAW THAT GUY WHO DRAWS THAT COMIC BOOK YOU LIKE.
YOU **SAW** HIM? WHERE?
HE WAS IN A COMIC SHOP, **WATCHING** PEOPLE READ **HIS** COMIC.
THAT'S **WEIRD.**

OH... AND I SAW YOUR **EX-GIRLFRIEND**, EVE. SHE WAS WITH SOME **NEW** GUY. DO YOU WANT A BEER?

YOU SAW **EVE?**
WHERE DID YOU SEE HER?
SHE WAS **WITH** SOMEONE ELSE?
HELLO?
ARE YOU LISTENING? **WHO** WAS EVE WITH?
I THINK THERE'S ANOTHER IN HERE SOMEWHERE.

THERE WASN'T A HERO IN THE MOVIE. I WOULDN'T WANT TO BE ANY OF THOSE CHARACTERS. EVERYONE WAS EITHER A VILLAIN OR VICTIM. YOU DIDN'T LIE, BUT YOU MANIPULATED HIM. DO YOU FEEL GUILTY ABOUT THAT?

I DON'T FEEL GUILTY. WE'RE BOTH HAPPIER THIS WAY. HI, KITTY.

PERSONALLY, I'D RATHER BE A VILLAIN THAN A VICTIM. BUT I GUESS IT'S EASIER MENTALLY FOR MOST PEOPLE TO SUFFER AS A VICTIM THAN TO DEAL WITH THE GUILT OF BEING A VILLAIN. AND IF YOU'RE NOT A VICTIM, THEN YOU'RE RESPONSIBLE FOR YOUR OWN LIFE. MOST PEOPLE DON'T WANT THAT KIND OF RESPONSIBILITY.

REMEMBER THE FIRST RULE OF DRINKING- "YOUR JUDGMENT IS IMPAIRED, SO YOU CAN'T JUDGE HOW MUCH YOUR JUDGMENT IS IMPAIRED."
I JUST WANT TO CALL HER.
HEY, TALK TO ME! GIVE SOME ATTENTION TO ME! HOW CAN AN ANIMAL WITH A BRAIN THE SIZE OF A WALNUT BE MORE INTERESTING THAN ME?
TRUST ME- DON'T DO IT. KEEP YOUR SELF-RESPECT. SUFFER THROUGH THIS DRUNKEN NIGHT, AND IT'LL BE BETTER TOMORROW. BESIDES, THEY SHUT MY PHONE OFF. I'M GOING TO BED. GOOD NIGHT.
YOU WOULDN'T DECEIVE ME LIKE YOU DID HIM, WOULD YOU?
OF COURSE NOT. LET'S GO TO BED.
DOES EVERYONE FEEL AS ALONE IN THE UNIVERSE AS I DO?
NOT REALLY. SEE YOU IN THE MORNING.
HELLO? EVE? ARE YOU AWAKE? I WANT TO TALK TO YOU. HELLO!
BANG BANG
SHE'S GOT A KEY HIDDEN AROUND HERE SOMEWHERE.
TO BE CONTINUED...

©1995 SHANNON WHEELER

I HOPE I'M NOT PREGNANT... AGAIN.

NO! HE DID ***NOT*** BEGIN AS A ***PRE-NATAL*** TRAILER PARK ***TRAGEDY!*** NOR WAS IT A ***GOVERNMENT EXPERIMENT*** THAT SIRED ***TOO MUCH COFFEE MAN.*** OUR STORY IS MORE ***COMPLICATED*** THAN THAT.

NO ALIENS WERE INVOLVED. EVEN THOUGH SOME PEOPLE THINK ***COFFEE BEANS*** ARE FROM ***OUTER SPACE.***

COULD HE HAVE BEEN A ***STUDENT,*** TRYING TO ***MEMORIZE*** COUNTLESS FACTS: ***OVERWHELMING*** TODAY AND ***IRRELEVANT*** TOMORROW. COULD ONE ***MORE*** CUP OF ***COFFEE*** MAKE ACADEMIA SEEM ***SIGNIFICANT?*** PERHAPS...

BUT ***THAT*** IS ***NOT*** HOW OUR HERO BEGAN. ***HOW*** DID ***TOO MUCH COFFEE MAN*** COME INTO BEING? WAS IT THE **CIA?**

OUR STORY ***DOES*** BEGIN, FINALLY, ***HERE***, IN A CAFÉ JUST OUTSIDE A SMALL TOWN.

HERE IT IS!!! THE SECRET ORIGIN OF OUR HERO, TOO MUCH COFFEE MAN, PRESENTED IN AN EASY-TO-UNDERSTAND FORMAT!!!
IT BEGINS IN A NEARBY HIGH SCHOOL WITH A TYPICAL ALIENATED YOUTH...
MY LIFE SUCKS. IT'S BORING. I'M BORING. I WISH SOMETHING WOULD HAPPEN. ANYTHING.
B22
DOOMED
THE ONLY THING THAT INSPIRES ME IS MY LOVE FOR LISA EVANS. ONLY, SHE DOESN'T EVEN KNOW MY NAME.
THAT CREEPY GUY ALWAYS STARES AT ME. I BET I COULD GET HIM TO DO MY HOMEWORK. HE LOOKS SMART. I WISH I COULD REMEMBER HIS NAME.
HI, I'M DOING TERRIBLE IN SCHOOL. I DON'T KNOW YOU-BUT MAYBE WE COULD MEET FOR COFFEE AND DO MY HOMEWORK.
SURE, I MEAN, THAT WOULD BE GREAT. I DON'T DRINK COFFEE. I MEAN, NOT YET, BUT I'LL DO ANYTHING FOR YOU, EVEN THOUGH I DON'T KNOW YOU AT ALL. MAYBE BECAUSE I DON'T KNOW YOU, I THINK YOU'RE SO GREAT. IF I DID KNOW YOU, PERHAPS I'D REALIZE WHAT A LOSER YOU ARE.
UH...OK...
GOOD, I'LL MEET YOU AT THE CAFÉ AFTER SCHOOL TODAY.

AFTER SCHOOL OUR HERO WALKS IN TO A SCENE DESTINED TO RADICALLY CHANGE HIS LIFE...
HE DOESN'T HAVE A CLUE AS TO HIS NEFARIOUS FATE.
COFFEE?
HELLO?

COFFEE?
I DON'T DRINK COFFEE! IT CAUSES ANXIETY, HEART PROBLEMS, MOOD SWINGS, YELLOW TEETH, FOUL BREATH, AND IT TASTES BAD!
WHY DO YOU WEAR A COFFEE MUG ON YOUR SHIRT IF YOU DON'T DRINK COFFEE?
IT'S NOT A COFFEE MUG, IT'S A TEACUP. THIS IS A TEA-SHIRT. IT'S A PUN.
WE DON'T GET MANY PUNS IN HERE.
I GOTTA GO STUDY.
MORE BEER?
SURE.

WAS THE WAITRESS MAKING A PUN?
TWO HOURS ISN'T BAD... SHE'S PROBABLY JUST HAVING A COUPLE BEERS AT SOME GUY'S HOUSE...

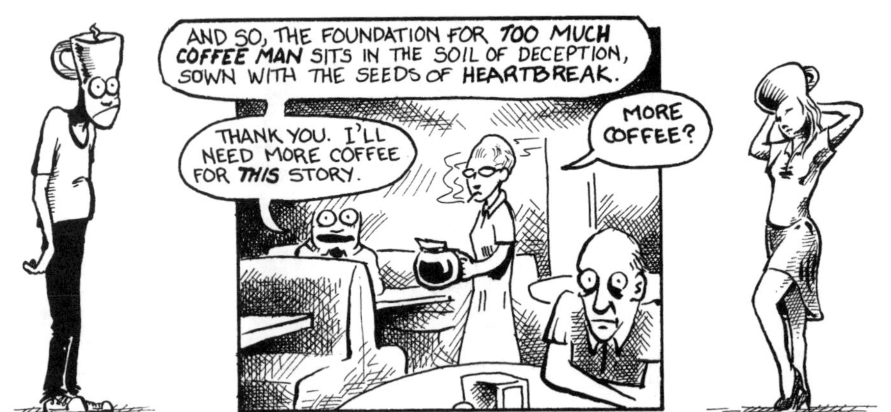
AND SO, THE FOUNDATION FOR TOO MUCH COFFEE MAN SITS IN THE SOIL OF DECEPTION, SOWN WITH THE SEEDS OF HEARTBREAK.
THANK YOU. I'LL NEED MORE COFFEE FOR THIS STORY.
MORE COFFEE?

BECAUSE THIS STORY INCLUDES A TRUCK DRIVER HEADING FOR A CENTRAL AMERICAN COFFEE FARM.

I'VE HAD TOO MUCH COFFEE. I'M GLAD I HAVE MY THERMOS.

HERE'S YOUR LOAD OF DDT. RIGHT ON SCHEDULE!
THANKS.
DO YOU HAVE A PLACE I CAN THROW AWAY MY THERMOS?
WHY DO YOU NEED ALL THIS DDT ANYWAY?
WE GOT SOME EXPERIMENTAL, GENETICALLY ENGINEERED COFFEE PLANTS. THEY'RE MORE CAFFEINATED. BUT THE INSECTS LOVE TO EAT THEM UP.

I CAN'T SELL DDT IN THE U.S. IT'S JUST TOO DANGEROUS.
I COULD GET FINED.
THAT'S WEIRD. WE SELL ALL OUR DDT-SPRAYED PRODUCT BACK TO THE U.S.

AND SO THE PLOT THICKENS LIKE DAY-OLD COFFEE. THE UNSUSPECTING PLANTS AND OUR OBLIVIOUS HERO ARE ON A COLLISION COURSE WITH DESTINY! IS IT A TRAGEDY? IS IT SERENDIPITY?
OR IS IT GRATUITOUS?

OOPS- DUMPED MY LOAD ALL IN ONE SPOT.

I'M SURE IT'LL SPREAD ITSELF OUT IN THE RAIN.

BUT THE RAIN DOESN'T "SPREAD IT OUT." IN FACT, THE RAIN CRYSTALLIZES THE DDT. AND IT'S NOT NORMAL RAIN, IT'S EVIL ACID RAIN!

SO THE ACID RAIN REACTS WITH THE DDT, FORMING NEW, UNPRECEDENTED CHEMICAL BONDS WITH THE UNSUSPECTING COFFEE BEANS.

MAKING A SUPER DEADLY POTENT COFFEE BEAN!

WHAT SHOULD I DO WITH THIS?
JUST CHIP OUT THE COFFEE BEANS.

THESE LITTLE PILES OF WHITE POWDER LOOK AMAZINGLY LIKE...
CHIP CHIP CHIP

NOBODY MOVE!
BAM
HUH?

RAT-A-TAT A-TAT A-TAT A-TAT

WHY DID YOU SHOOT?
IT LOOKED LIKE HE MOVED.
TECHNICALLY YOU CAN'T HELP BUT MOVE A LITTLE.
WE'RE MIGHTY TOUGH.
YEAH.

DON'T YOU THINK IT STRANGE THAT THE LARGEST FARMER AROUND GIVES US SO MANY DRUG TIPS ABOUT THE OTHER SMALLER COMPETING FARMERS?
NO. IT'S VERY TYPICAL FOR THIS TYPE OF SITUATION.
LET'S GET OUT OF HERE!
FIRST, LOAD SOME "COFFEE BEANS" FOR THE "MORNING."
AND WE MIGHT AS WELL GET SOME COFFEE BEANS FOR THE MORNING, TOO.

WHAT'S THAT TICKING NOISE?
I DON'T KNOW, BUT IT SOUNDS LIKE...
TICK TICK TICK TICK TICK TICK

COSMIC RADIATION!!!

I-I FEEL AS IF A MILLION TINY NEEDLES ARE PIERCING MY BODY...
NO TIME TO BE TRENDY! WE'VE GOT TO TAKE THIS COPTER DOWN FAST!

ARG! WE'VE FLOWN TOO LOW TOO FAST! WE'VE ACCIDENTALLY FLOWN INTO... A...

A NEVADA NUCLEAR TESTING SITE!!!
FOOMP

THAT WAS TOO CLOSE FOR COMFORT!
I'M UNCOMFOR-TABLE.

MEANWHILE
UH, WAITRESS, I'VE CHANGED MY MIND. I THINK I WILL HAVE THAT COFFEE.
WE JUST RAN OUT. I'LL MAKE A NEW POT. IT'LL JUST BE A SEC.

HEY, JOE! WE'RE OUT OF COFFEE! GO GET SOME MORE BEANS!
IT'LL JUST BE A MINUTE.
MEANWHILE. THE SPY PLANE, ITS OCCUPANTS, AND THE RADIOACTIVE COFFEEARE IN DEEP TROUBLE.
IF WE'RE GOING TO SURVIVE THIS, WE'VE GOT TO JETTISON CARGO.
OUT OF COFFEE? DAMN, THOSE FREE REFILLS DURING POETRY READINGS ARE KILLING ME. NOW, WHERE CAN I GET COFFEE THIS LATE?
HEY. LOOK AT THAT. IT'S A SECRET SPY PLANE DROPPING BAGS OF COFFEE RIGHT OUTSIDE MY CAFÉ.
COFFEE
IT'S AS THOUGH THE HAND OF FATE REACHED DOWN AND HANDED ME A GIFT HORSE.
COFFEE
STRANGE. THESE BEANS SEEM TO GLOW- AS IF THEY'RE IMBUED WITH SOME SPECIAL POWER.
COFFEE
DON'T WORRY. YOU'LL GET YOURS SOON.
OH, GOOD.

SO. THE ELEMENTS SLIP INTO PLACE. READY TO PLAY THEIR PUNY PARTS IN THIS DIAPHANOUS DRAMA. THIS CAUSTIC COMEDY. THIS TEDIOUS TRAGEDY. THIS ILLITERATE ALLITERATION.
SHE'S FIVE HOURS LATE.
BUT I'M SURE SHE'LL SEE HOW MUCH SHE NEEDS ME... ONCE SHE SOBERS UP... AND NEEDS HELP WITH HER HOMEWORK.
I THINK I'LL TAKE UP SMOKING.
ALIENATION IS FERTILE GROUND FOR CREATION... ESPECIALLY WHEN MIXED WITH COFFEE MADE FROM RADIOACTIVE BEANS.
ONE POTENT CUP OF COFFEE!
CAREFUL. IT'S HOT.
SIMPLY SMELLING THIS COFFEE MAKES ME AWARE OF THE LIMITLESS POTENTIAL IN MY LIFE. MY BEAUTIFUL LIFE! IN THIS WONDERFUL CAFÉ! I'M GLAD I WAS STOOD UP!
TO THINK, SO MUCH FEELING IN A SIMPLE CUP OF COFFEE!
NORMAL COFFEE GIVES PEOPLE A TEMPORARY, MILD EUPHORIC BUZZ. BUT THIS IS SUPER COFFEE...
EXPOSED TO DDT, RADIATION, GENETIC ENGINEERING, AND A DRIP-BREWING PROCESS. IT IS COSMIC COFFEE! STRONG ENOUGH TO TURN ONE INTO A JITTERY SUPERHERO!
TOXIC ENOUGH TO KILL ANYONE STUPID ENOUGH TO DRINK IT.

YES! THE CAUSTIC COFFEE KILLED HIM! WHILE I, YOUR HUMBLE NARRATOR, SAT AND WATCHED THE DEADLY EVENTS UNFOLD. I COULD HAVE DONE SOMETHING TO AVERT THE TRAGEDY. I DID NOTHING! I DRANK CUP AFTER CUP OF COFFEE. IN FACT, I DRANK TOO MUCH COFFEE!

THAT'S RIGHT! I AM TOO MUCH COFFEE MAN!
RIP

OH, WAITRESS, I WOULD LIKE ANOTHER REFILL PLEASE.
YOU'LL HAVE TO LEAVE. I HAVE A PUDDLE-OF-A-PERSON TO MOP UP. BESIDES, YOU'VE HAD TOO MUCH COFFEE.

OF COURSE I'VE HAD TOO MUCH COFFEE!

I'M TOO MUCH COFFEE MAN.
PLEASE LEAVE.

DONE!
RING
RING
HELLO?... OH, HEY, WHAT'S UP?... I'M JUST FINISHING UP THE ORIGIN STORY... I DON'T KNOW... I HOPE PEOPLE LIKE IT. LORD KNOWS I PUT ENOUGH WORK IN IT.
THAT'S TRUE, HEH, HEH... MAYBE NEXT TIME I'LL WORK LESS... YOU ARE? I HAVE A RADIO INTERVIEW, BUT I SHOULD BE DONE BY THEN.
OH, MAN. IT'S LATE. I HAVE TO GET DRESSED FOR THIS THING... HEH, HEH, I GUESS I DON'T HAVE TO DRESS FOR RADIO... SEE YOU AT THREE... 'BYE.

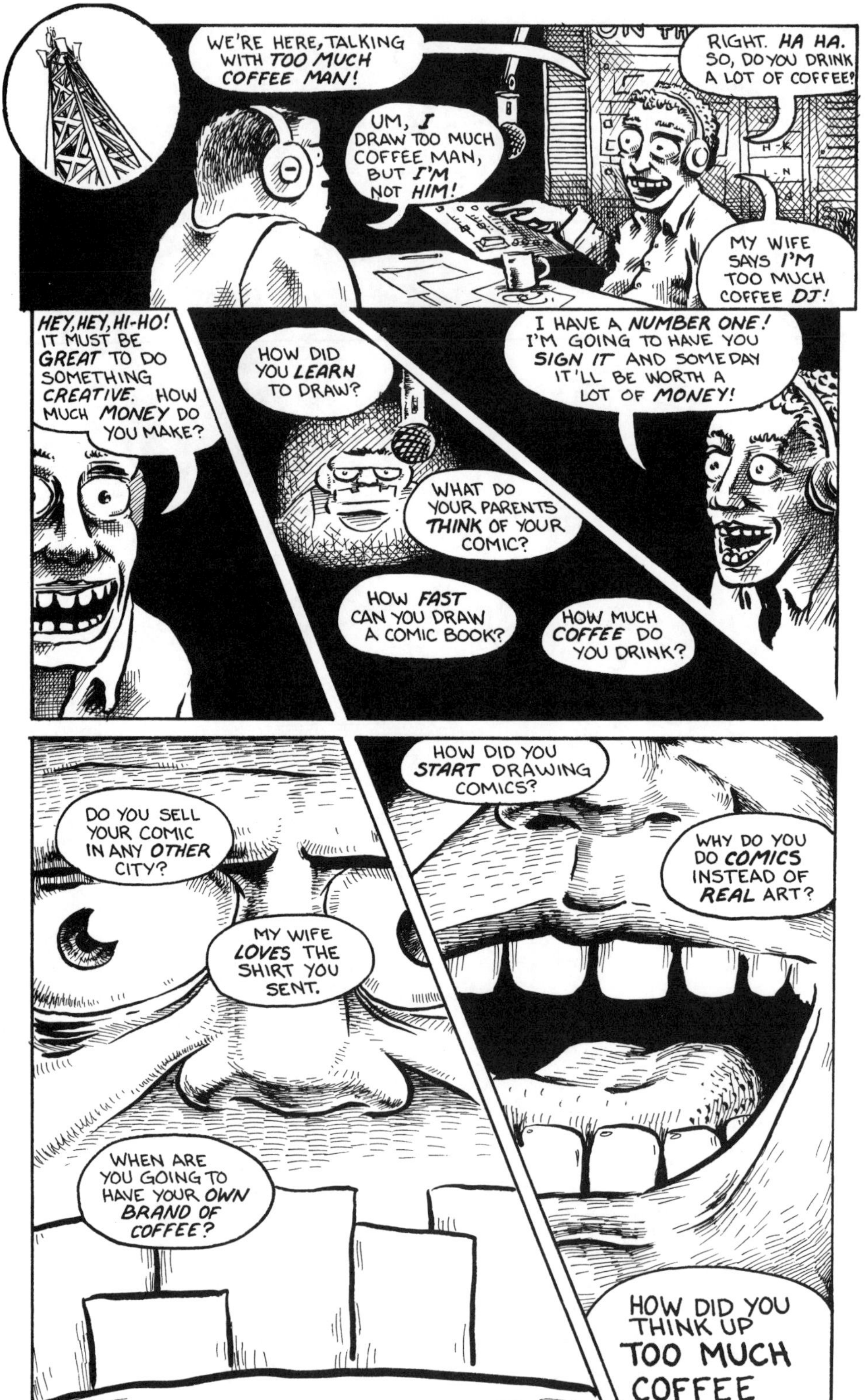

WE'RE HERE, TALKING WITH TOO MUCH COFFEE MAN!

UM, I DRAW TOO MUCH COFFEE MAN, BUT I'M NOT HIM!

RIGHT. HA HA. SO, DO YOU DRINK A LOT OF COFFEE?

MY WIFE SAYS I'M TOO MUCH COFFEE DJ!

HEY, HEY, HI-HO! IT MUST BE GREAT TO DO SOMETHING CREATIVE. HOW MUCH MONEY DO YOU MAKE?

HOW DID YOU LEARN TO DRAW?

I HAVE A NUMBER ONE! I'M GOING TO HAVE YOU SIGN IT AND SOMEDAY IT'LL BE WORTH A LOT OF MONEY!

WHAT DO YOUR PARENTS THINK OF YOUR COMIC?

HOW FAST CAN YOU DRAW A COMIC BOOK?

HOW MUCH COFFEE DO YOU DRINK?

DO YOU SELL YOUR COMIC IN ANY OTHER CITY?

MY WIFE LOVES THE SHIRT YOU SENT.

WHEN ARE YOU GOING TO HAVE YOUR OWN BRAND OF COFFEE?

HOW DID YOU START DRAWING COMICS?

WHY DO YOU DO COMICS INSTEAD OF REAL ART?

HOW DID YOU THINK UP TOO MUCH COFFEE MAN?

YOU ACTUALLY WANT ME TO ANSWER A QUESTION?
HA HA, OF COURSE.
I USED TO DRAW A COMIC STRIP FOR MY COLLEGE PAPER. IT WAS ABOUT RELATIONSHIPS.
I WAS IN A CAFÉ, TRYING TO COME UP WITH A CARTOON THAT WOULD BE MORE POPULAR.
THE MAGICIAN
TOOTH & JUSTICE
A FRIEND DID A COMIC MOCKING THE POPULAR STRIPS-HOW THEY RELY ON SIMPLE ICONOGRAPHY FOR QUICK RECOGNITION.
I STARTED WORKING ON A CHARACTER WITH A SIMPLE HOOK OR HANDLE SO IT COULD BE POPULAR.
A HANDLE FOR EASY RECOGNITION. IT WAS A PUN!
YOU TRIED TO THINK UP SOMETHING POPULAR. AND ACTUALLY DID?
WOW. THAT DOESN'T SOUND VERY ARTISTIC.
IT'S NOT THAT POPULAR.
WHEN'S THE NEXT ISSUE COMING OUT?
SOON.
IS THERE GOING TO BE A CARTOON?
I JUST STARTED TALKING TO A SMALL ANIMATION COMPANY.
THANKS FOR COMING DOWN!... WE'VE BEEN TALKING TO TOO MUCH COFFEE MAN!
CAN I GET A MUG FOR MY WIFE?
THERE IT IS — THE DUBIOUS ORIGIN OF TOO MUCH COFFEE MAN! YOU ARE TUNED TO K.R.E.D. 90.7 FM, ON THE FAR LEFT OF YOUR RADIO DIAL: "BETTER RED THAN DEAD." THANK YOU AND GOOD NIGHT.

RUMBLE RUMBLE RUMBLE
HEY! OVER HERE!
OPEN
HOW DID YOUR RADIO INTERVIEW TURN OUT?
SAME OLD QUESTIONS. SAME OLD JOKES. HE MADE FUN OF MY CLOTHES. I'M GETTING A COFFEE.
YAH. I WISH I HAD A BETTER STORY. BUT I WAS JUST TELLING THE TRUTH.
COULD I GET ONE LARGE, STEAMING HOT CAPPUCCINO, PLEASE?
DID YOU TELL THE STORY OF COMING UP WITH TOO MUCH COFFEE MAN AS A WAY TO GET POPULAR?
PEOPLE ARE GOING TO STOP LIKING YOUR STUFF IF THEY THINK IT'S SOMETHING PHONY.
YOU MEAN, I NEED TO BE PHONY SO PEOPLE WILL THINK I'M SINCERE?

WHO DO YOU DRAW FOR?
I DRAW FOR FEMINISM! TO SHOW THAT WOMEN ARE STRONG AND POWERFUL. I WANT TO MOCK THE HYPOCRISY INNATE TO THE MALE PARADIGM.
NO, NO. I MEAN, WHO DO YOU IMAGINE WATCHING YOU AS YOU DRAW?
I DON'T KNOW... I GUESS I HAVE AN IMAGINARY PERSON I DRAW FOR. I HADN'T THOUGHT ABOUT IT BEFORE.
SOMETIMES IT HELPS ME TO PICTURE A GHOSTLY FIGURE WATCHING ME DRAW. LIKE A STRONG AND LOVING GUARDIAN ANGEL WHO BATHES ME IN WAVES OF APPROVAL. OF COURSE, I WAS RAISED CATHOLIC.
I THINK OF MY FAMILY. ESPECIALLY MY BROTHER. IF I CAN SEE HIM LAUGHING, THEN I'M HAPPY.
WOW. THAT'S SO NICE. WHAT ABOUT YOU?
I IMAGINE MYSELF AT THE CENTER OF AN ENORMOUS ARENA PACKED TO CAPACITY WITH MY FANS. AN IMAGE OF WHAT I'M DRAWING BEAMS FROM GIANT TEE-VEES AT EITHER END OF THE STADIUM. AND EVERYONE CHEERS EACH TIME I DRAW A REALLY GOOD LINE.
YOU'RE WEIRD.

WOULD YOU RATHER BE RICH OR FAMOUS?
RICH, THEN YOU'D BE FREE TO DO YOUR ART WITHOUT WORRY.
YOU NEED SOME FAME BECAUSE PEOPLE NEED TO SEE WHAT YOU'RE DOING. ART IS A RELATIONSHIP OF CREATOR AND AUDIENCE.
IF YOU HAVE FAME, YOU CAN ALWAYS MAKE MONEY. LOOK AT ALL THE FAMOUS HACKS.
WOULD YOU RATHER BE THE GUY DOING THE WORK, AND GET NO CREDIT- OR GET THE CREDIT, NOT HAVING DONE THE WORK?
WHO GETS THE MONEY?
THE BUSINESSMEN MAKE MONEY. YOU NEVER GET RICH WORKING FOR SOMEONE ELSE. THAT'S WHY SO MANY PEOPLE ARE SELF-PUBLISHING.
I WANT TO HAVE MY ARTISTIC CAREER AND EAT TOO!
I WANT TO HAVE MY CAKE, EAT IT, AND THEN SELL IT NATIONALLY.
ARE YOU GOING TO EAT THAT CAKE?
YES, I'M GOING TO EAT IT!

I FEEL SICK.
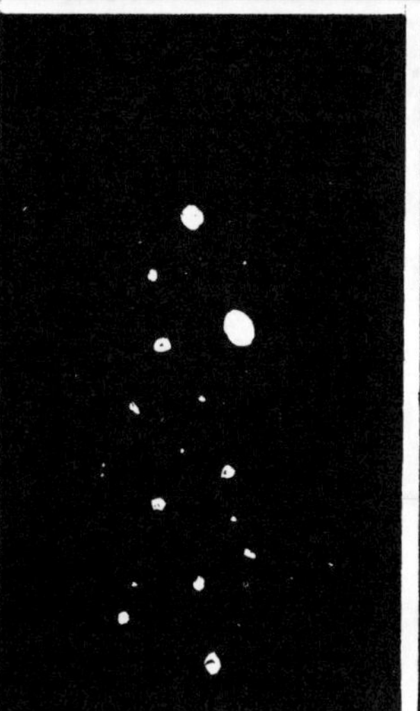

REMEMBER, YOU'RE DRUNK! DRUNKS DO STUPID THINGS THAT THEY'RE ASHAMED OF LATER. SUFFER THROUGH, CONTROL YOUR IMPULSES. KEEP YOUR DIGNITY!

EVE, I JUST WANT TO TALK TO YOU!

BANG
CLATTER
CLATTER

TOO MUCH COFFEE

SHE THREW AWAY MY COMIC BOOKS.

UH-OH. MY MOUTH IS ALL **WATERY**. PLEASE, I DON'T WANT TO **THROW UP**.

BUURP
SPLASH

AT LEAST NOW I **FEEL** BETTER.

I DON'T **UNDERSTAND**. I'M SO **DRUNK**, BUT THINGS SEEM SO **CLEAR**.
STUMBLE
RETCH

I **NEVER** THOUGHT **CEMENT** COULD BE SO **COMFORTABLE**.

SHOULD I CALL THE **POLICE**?
SURE.

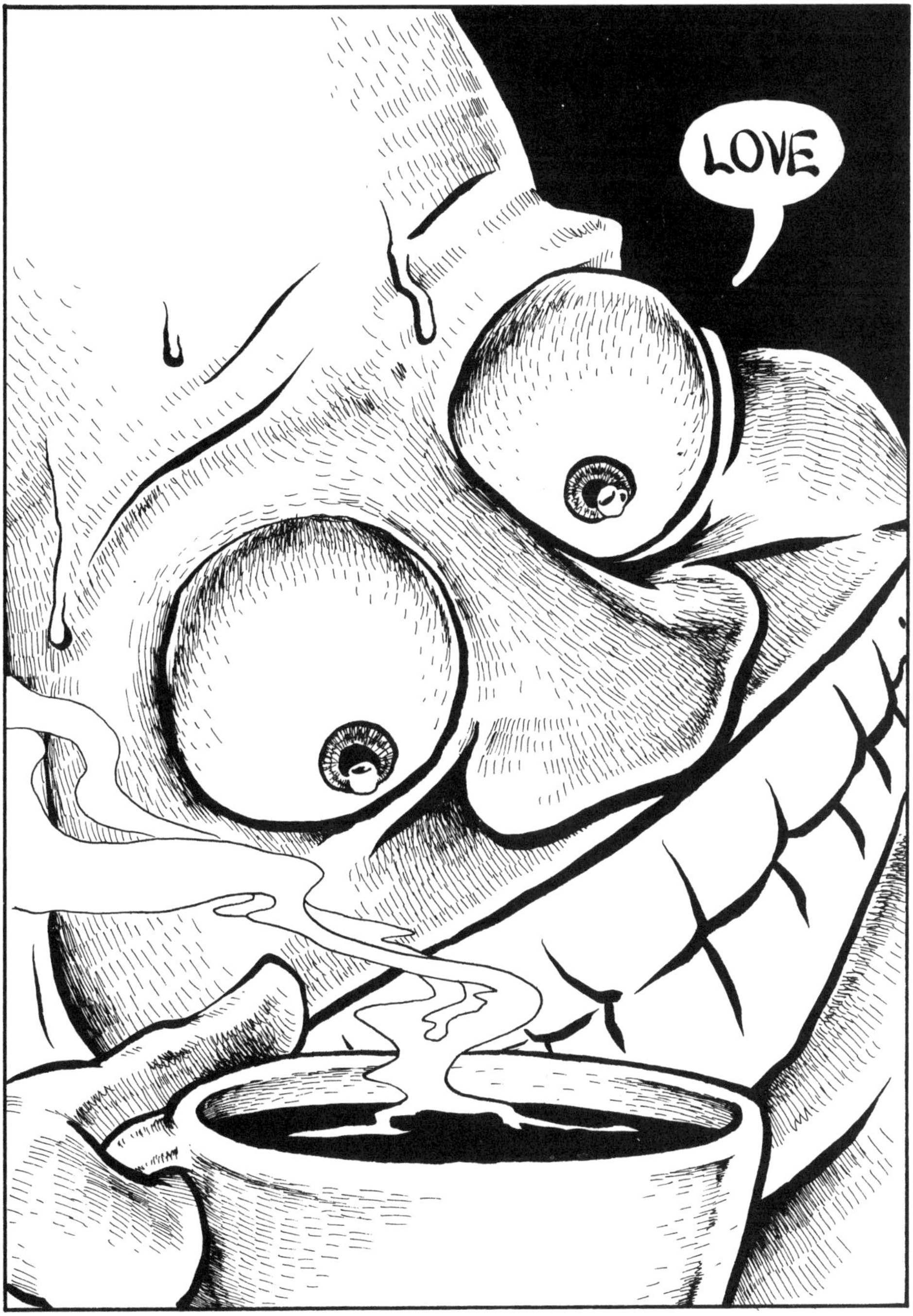

LOVE

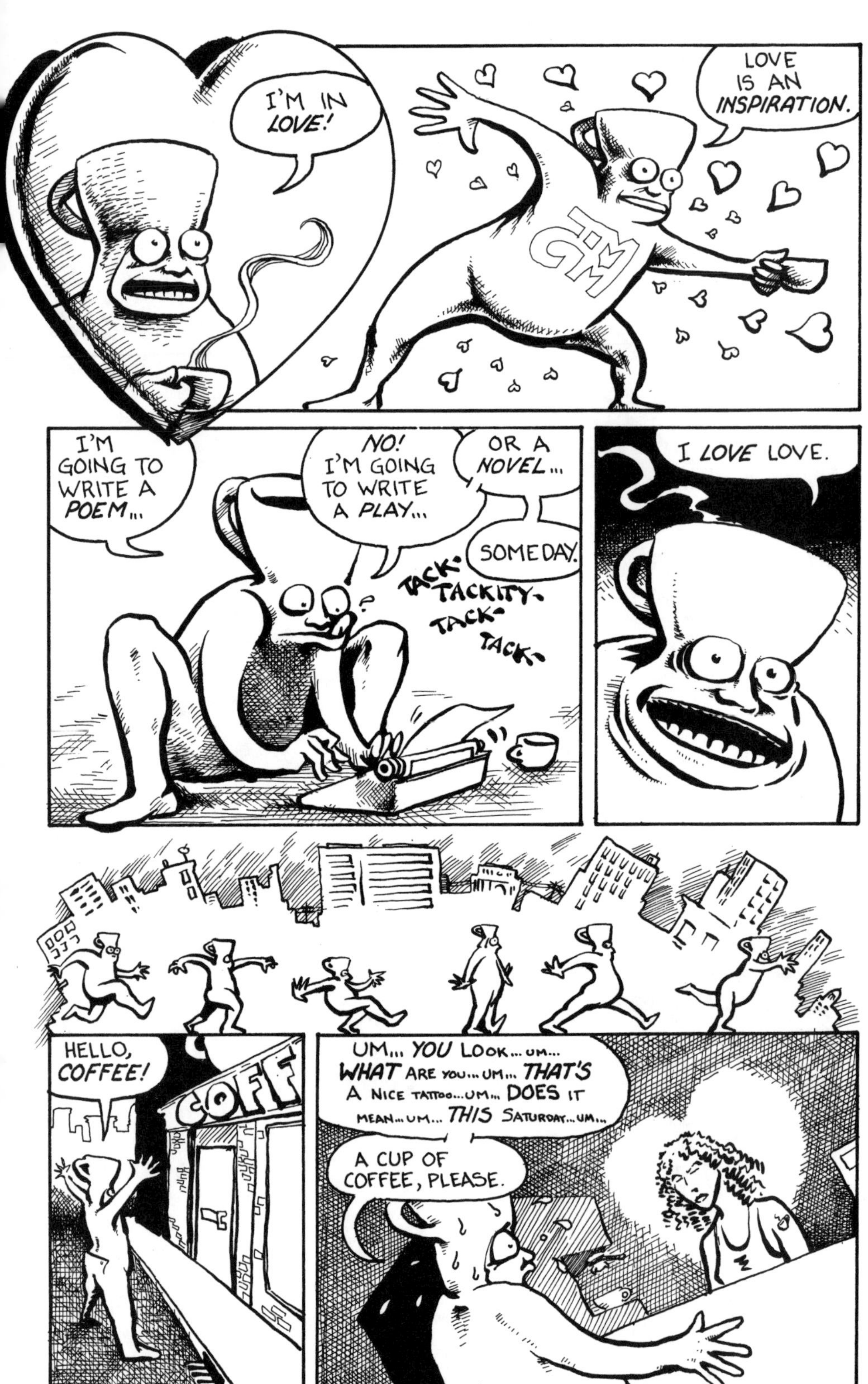

I'M IN LOVE!
LOVE IS AN INSPIRATION.
I'M GOING TO WRITE A POEM...
NO! I'M GOING TO WRITE A PLAY...
OR A NOVEL...
SOMEDAY.
TACK-TACKITY-TACK-TACK-
I LOVE LOVE.
HELLO, COFFEE!
COFF
UM... YOU LOOK... UM... WHAT ARE YOU... UM... THAT'S A NICE TATTOO... UM... DOES IT MEAN... UM... THIS SATURDAY... UM...
A CUP OF COFFEE, PLEASE.

I LOVE THAT COFFEE GIRL. BUT WHY CAN'T I TALK TO HER?
I HATE LOVE.

I CAN TELL A CUP OF COFFEE EVERY SECRET IN MY SOUL– AND EXPRESS MY TOTAL LOVE.
I DO LOVE YOU, LITTLE CUP OF COFFEE.

WHY AM I SUCH AN IDIOT IN FRONT OF THE GIRL I LOVE?

BECAUSE A CUP OF COFFEE IS AN INANIMATE OBJECT, WHILE A PERSON CAN REJECT YOU. AND REJECTION IS SCARY!

THANK YOU, LITTLE CUP OF COFFEE.
I GUESS I'M DONE WITH YOU.

YIKES
HELLO.
YOU LOOK FAMILIAR. DO I KNOW YOU FROM SOMEWHERE? WHAT ARE YOU STUDYING? THAT'S A NICE TATTOO. DOES IT MEAN SOMETHING? WHEN DO YOU GET OFF WORK? WHAT ARE YOU DOING THIS SATURDAY?
YOU'RE REALLY PATHETIC! PEOPLE LIKE YOU MAKE ME SICK! YOU'RE A FAKE AND A PHONY!
I AM NOT PAID ENOUGH TO DEAL WITH THIS SORT OF GARBAGE!
IN FACT, I HATE YOU AND I HATE THIS PLACE!
TAPOW

SMASH!

STOP THIS *DESTRUCTION*! YOU'RE DIRECTING YOUR ANGER IN THE *WRONG* WAY!

WHAT ARE YOU TALKING ABOUT? I *HATE* MY JOB, I *HATE* MY BOSS, AND I *HATE* THESE PEOPLE!

THIS IS THE *PERFECT* PLACE TO SMASH UP!

OOOOOF!

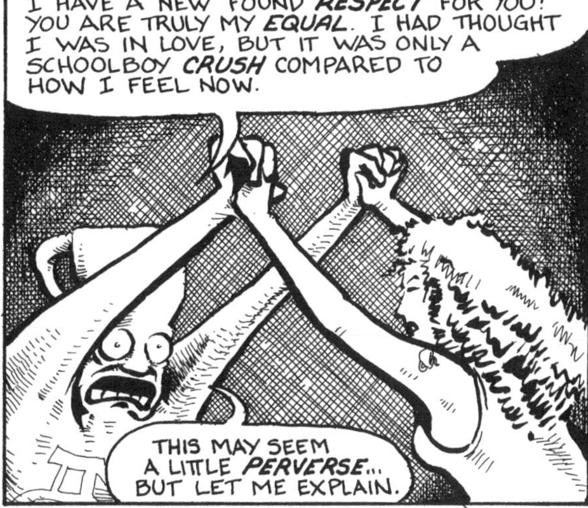

I WANT YOU TO JOIN ME IN MY ADVENTURES AND BE MY *SIDEKICK!*
BE THE *FILTER* FOR MY BEAN! BE THE *CREAM* FOR MY COFFEE!
FLING
CRASH
BE...TOO MUCH COFFEE *WOMAN!*
YOU CAN DRESS IN A *COOL* COSTUME, AND WE'LL TRAVEL THE WORLD, FIGHTING CRIME AND DOING *STUFF.*
WE CAN TAKE TURNS *SAVING* EACH OTHER FROM UNLIKELY AND PERILOUS SITUATIONS.
I NEED A *SIDEKICK!*

REJECT ME NOW. I'VE HAD THE CHANCE TO EXPRESS MYSELF, AND A WEIGHT HAS BEEN LIFTED FROM MY SOUL.
I'VE COME TO THIS CAFÉ FOR WEEKS JUST TO SEE YOU. BUT UNTIL NOW I'VE BEEN TOO SCARED TO TALK TO YOU.
REALLY?
HEY, ME TOO!
I LOVE HER TOO.
I DON'T EVEN LIKE COFFEE.
YEAH, ME TOO.
I WAS COMING HERE TO SEE HER BEFORE YOU WERE.
THAT EXPLAINS WHY THIS JOB WAS SO CREEPY. YOU PEOPLE ARE THE LAMEST EXCUSE FOR HUMAN BEINGS EVER!
FURTHER-MORE, WHO NEEDS YOU TO BE A SUPERHERO? I CAN BE ONE ON MY OWN!
SLAM!
WOW. THAT WAS HARSH.

I'M HAPPY BECAUSE I KNOW THAT AT LEAST YOU LOVE ME AND I LOVE ME.

YOU BETCHA.

THE END

I'M *MISERABLE*.

I USED TO HAVE A *LIFE*...

I READ BOOKS, SAW MOVIES, AND ENJOYED THE COMPANY OF WOMEN.

I GAVE IT ***ALL*** UP TO DRAW COMICS.

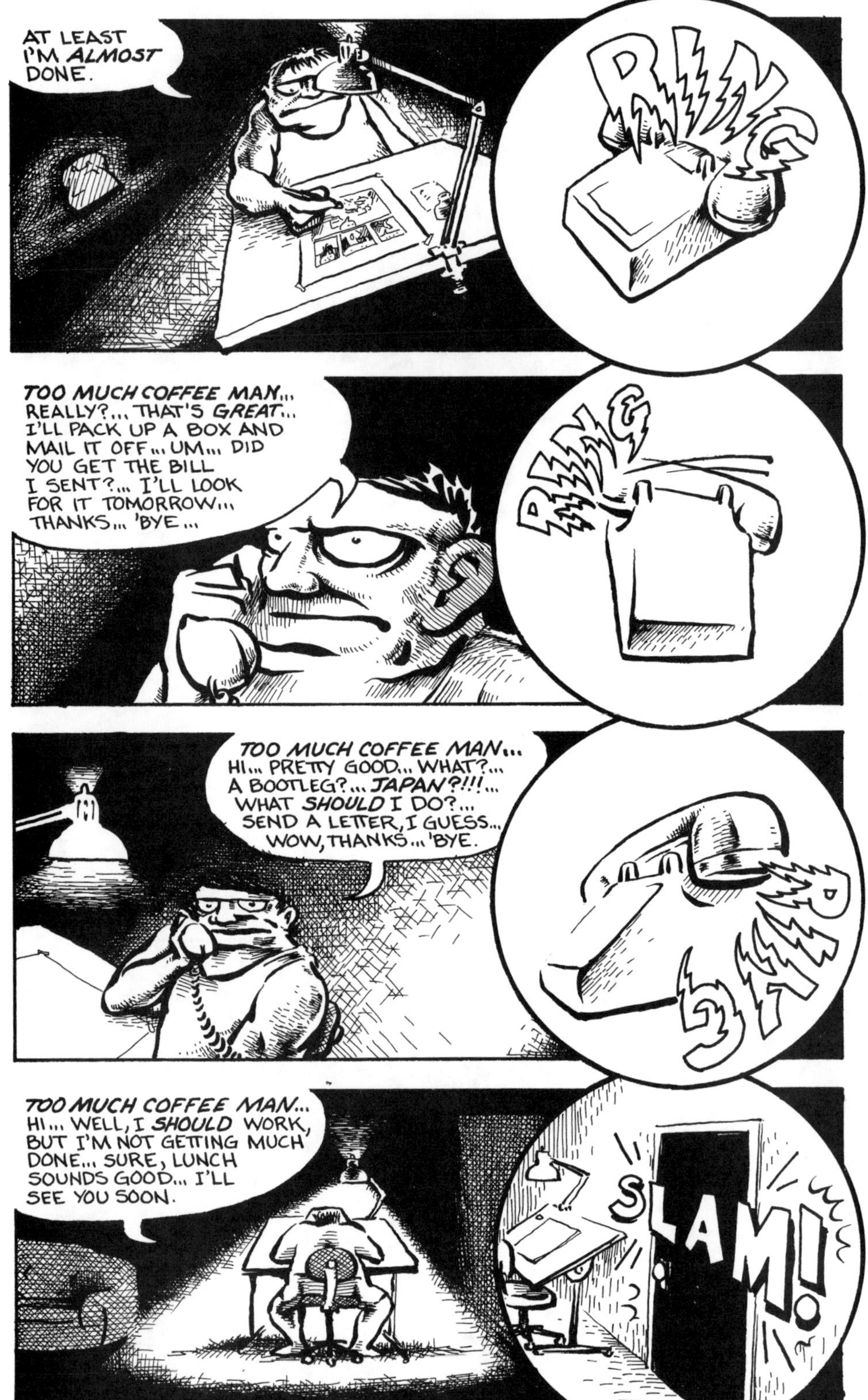
AT LEAST I'M *ALMOST* DONE.
RING
TOO MUCH COFFEE MAN... REALLY?... THAT'S *GREAT*... I'LL PACK UP A BOX AND MAIL IT OFF... UM... DID YOU GET THE BILL I SENT?... I'LL LOOK FOR IT TOMORROW... THANKS... 'BYE...
RING
TOO MUCH COFFEE MAN... HI... PRETTY GOOD... WHAT?... A BOOTLEG?... *JAPAN*?!!!... WHAT *SHOULD* I DO?... SEND A LETTER, I GUESS... WOW, THANKS... 'BYE.
RING
TOO MUCH COFFEE MAN... HI... WELL, I *SHOULD* WORK, BUT I'M NOT GETTING MUCH DONE... SURE, LUNCH SOUNDS GOOD... I'LL SEE YOU SOON.
SLAM!

I'LL HAVE A BEER AND A GREEK SALAD.
I'LL HAVE THE SAME.
WHERE'S YOUR CAR?
IT'S IN THE SHOP. I NEED A NEW CAR.
HOW'S GRAD SCHOOL?
I'M UP TO MY NECK IN BOOKS AND UP TO MY NOSE IN BILLS.
I SEE YOUR COMIC ALL OVER THE PLACE. YOU'RE DOING WELL.
I WORK ALL THE TIME.
THE MORE MONEY I EARN, THE MORE I NEED TO SPEND: CAR, PHONE, PRINTING, ADVERTISING, TRAVEL, DENTIST, AND DOCTOR. EVERYTHING TO MAKE LIFE AND BUSINESS BETTER.
I'M NICKLED AND DIMED BY CONVENIENCE.
I STILL THINK OF YOU AS A STRUGGLING ARTIST–IT'S HARD FOR ME TO IMAGINE YOU AS A SUCCESSFUL ARTIST.
CARTOONIST.
WHAT-EVER. DO YOU WANT TO GO SHOPPING?
DO YOU EVER THINK ABOUT YOUR AUDIENCE?
ALL THE TIME.
END

BOOZE
BAR

BOOB

OH, YOU'LL *TALK* ABOUT WRITING SCREENPLAYS, AND YOU'LL *TALK* ABOUT HOW, YOURS WILL BE *BETTER* THAN EVERYONE ELSE'S, BUT ONCE YOU START *WORKING* YOU'LL SEE HOW *HARD* IT *REALLY* IS, AND YOU WON'T *DO* ANYTHING.

SURE I WILL. YOU KNOW WHY? BECAUSE I'M IN *THIS* COMIC BOOK!

YOU WISH. YOU TALK LOUD, HOPING THAT PEOPLE ARE LISTENING TO YOU.

I HATE ALL THESE PEOPLE.
BECAUSE THEY REMIND YOU OF YOURSELF.

HEY, LISTEN, THEY'RE PLAYING THAT BROWN-EYED GIRL SONG YOU LIKE.

YOU KNOW WHAT THAT SONG IS REALLY ABOUT, DON'T YOU?

IT'S ABOUT AN INTERRACIAL RELATIONSHIP.
NOPE. IT'S ABOUT BUTT-SEX!

BEHIND THE STADIUM... DOWN IN THE HOLLOW, PLAYING A NEW GAME... HIDING BEHIND THE RAINBOW'S WALL... SLIPPIN' 'N' SLIDIN'...

TO BE CONTINUED...

I DON'T EVEN KNOW THIS GUY.

I LIKE FUNERALS.
YOU DRESS FANCY, EAT GOOD FOOD, AND THERE'S NO PRESSURE TO ENJOY YOURSELF.
WHEN I DIE, I WANT AN APPLE TREE PLANTED OVER MY HEAD. PEOPLE WILL EAT THE APPLES, THINK OF ME, AND BE EATING PART OF ME.
I THINK IT'S OVER.
I LIKED THE MOURNERS. THEY WERE A NICE TOUCH.
PERFORMANCE ART IS ALWAYS A HIT-OR-MISS AFFAIR.
MORE LIKE MISS, MISS, MISS, HIT, MISS, MISS, MISS, MISS, MISS.
THE IDEA WASN'T THAT BAD. A FUNERAL FOR THINGS DEAD: COMMUNISM, REAL DEMOCRACY, PRIVACY, 8-TRACK TAPES...
IT WOULD HAVE BEEN BETTER AS A CARTOON.
THE WHOLE IDEA COULD HAVE BEEN EXPRESSED IN A SINGLE PANEL.
SOME PEOPLE WOULD SAY THE SAME THING ABOUT YOUR COMIC BOOK.
AT LEAST WITH MY COMIC THEY CAN READ IT IN THE STORE AND THEY DON'T WASTE TWO HOURS AND SEVEN BUCKS.
I NEED TO GET BACK TO WORK.
I THINK YOU SHOULD KILL TOO MUCH COFFEE MAN.

AAAAARG!!!
MY *HEART!*

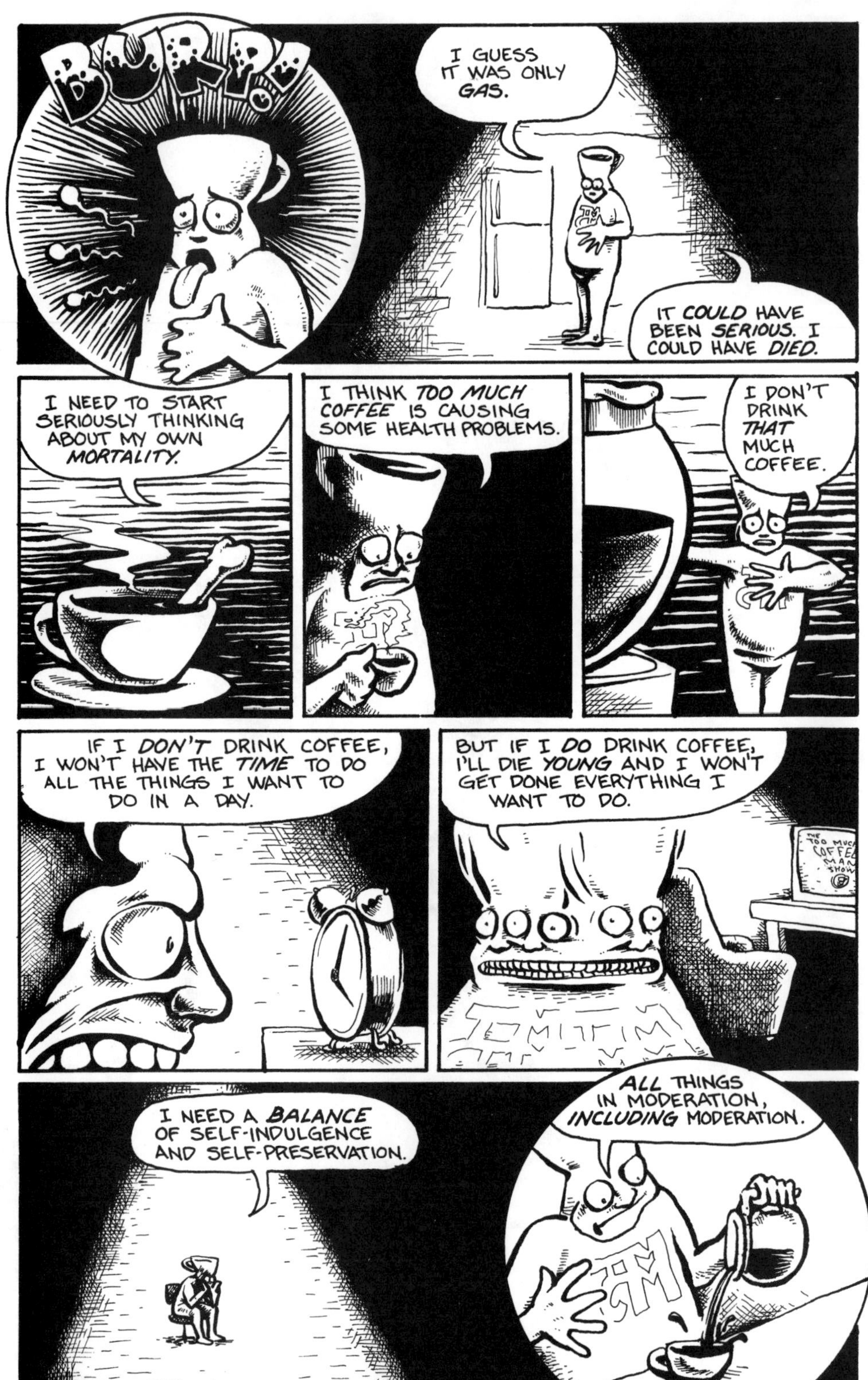
BURP!
I GUESS IT WAS ONLY GAS.
IT COULD HAVE BEEN SERIOUS. I COULD HAVE DIED.
I NEED TO START SERIOUSLY THINKING ABOUT MY OWN MORTALITY.
I THINK TOO MUCH COFFEE IS CAUSING SOME HEALTH PROBLEMS.
I DON'T DRINK THAT MUCH COFFEE.
IF I DON'T DRINK COFFEE, I WON'T HAVE THE TIME TO DO ALL THE THINGS I WANT TO DO IN A DAY.
BUT IF I DO DRINK COFFEE, I'LL DIE YOUNG AND I WON'T GET DONE EVERYTHING I WANT TO DO.
I NEED A BALANCE OF SELF-INDULGENCE AND SELF-PRESERVATION.
ALL THINGS IN MODERATION, INCLUDING MODERATION.

GOOD MORNING!

WHAT A BEAUTIFUL DAY!

I CAN'T BEGIN TO DESCRIBE HOW HAPPY I AM.

I AM SO HAPPY I COULD DIE.

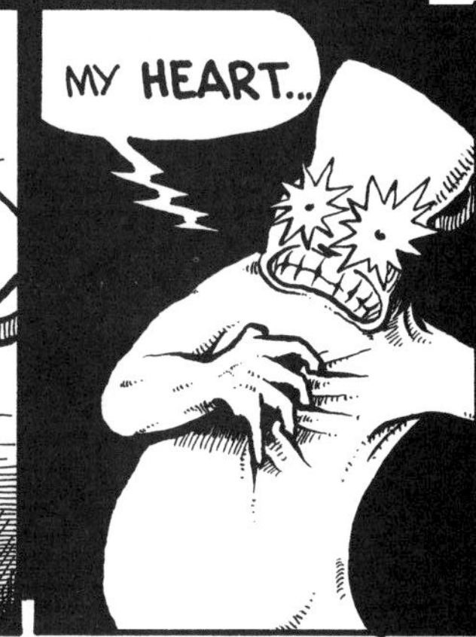
MY HEART...

DRAMATIC DEATH SCENE.

POOR TMCM... ONE CUP TOO MANY.
MUGS AND T-SHIRTS NOW AVAILABLE.

TOO MUCH COFFEE MAN IS DEAD?
TOO MUCH COFFEE MAN IS DEAD?
TOO MUCH COFFEE MAN IS DEAD?
TOO MUCH COFFEE MAN IS DEAD?
TOO MUCH COFFEE MAN IS DEAD!
TOO MUCH COFFEE MAN
TOO MUCH COFFEE MAN IS DEAD?
TOO MUCH COFFEE MAN IS DEAD?
TOO MUCH COFFEE MAN IS DEAD?
TOO MUCH COFFEE MAN IS DEAD?

WHAT HAS HAPPENED TO

TOO MUCH COFFEE MAN?

SINCE HE'S

DEAD!

IS TOO MUCH COFFEE MAN IN *HEAVEN*?

OR HAS HE BECOME A *SPIRIT*, WANDERING THE EARTH, INHABITING HAPLESS HOSTS?

IS HE TRAPPED IN *LIMBO*?

OR HAS HE GONE TO *HELL*?

WHAT *HAS* HAPPENED TO HIM?

WHAT?

WHAT?

WHAT?

MAYBE HE'S STILL ALIVE... ***BURIED ALIVE!***

BUT, TRAGICALLY, TOO MUCH COFFEE MAN IS *REALLY* DEAD,

AND *EVERYONE* GETS A COFFEE MUG.

NOW THAT HE'S GONE, I GUESS WE CAN START TALKING ABOUT HOW GREAT HE WAS.
SOMEONE'S AT THE DOOR.
EEEEEEEK!
TOO MUCH COFFEE MAN! YOU'RE ALIVE?!!!
UM... YEAH... SURE... I'M ALIVE... I GUESS.
HOW ARE YOU ALIVE?
UM... IT'S COMPLICATED.
I'M GONNA HAVE A CUP OF COFFEE.
WHERE IS MY COFFEE? WHERE ARE MY MUGS? WHERE IS ALL OF MY STUFF?
YOU CAME BACK FROM THE DEAD, AND ALL YOU CARE ABOUT IS A CUP OF COFFEE AND YOUR STUFF???
UM... YES.

TOO MUCH COFFEE MAN, WE THOUGHT YOU WERE DEAD!

UM... YEAH... WELL... SORT OF...

THERE WAS A MAD SCIENTIST WHO REMOVED MY BRAIN AND FROZE IT.

THEN MY BODY WAS CLONED...

AND SPACE ALIENS...

AND STUFF.

...YOU'RE NOT RESENTFUL THAT I CAME BACK FROM THE DEAD, ARE YOU?

IT IS SORT OF WEIRD.

AND IF ANYONE CAME BACK FROM THE DEAD, I WAS HOPING IT WOULD BE ME.

WHEN TOO MUCH COFFEE MAN DIED, I WAS REALLY SAD.
I SPENT A LOT OF TIME COMING TO TERMS WITH MY FEELINGS.
THEN, HE WASN'T DEAD.
AND I HAD TO COME TO TERMS WITH COMING TO TERMS WITH MY FEELINGS.
THEN, HE FELL OUT A WINDOW.
IT WAS A LONG FALL.
AND TOO MUCH COFFEE MAN IS DEAD AGAIN.
I GUESS THAT MEANS I NEED TO COME TO TERMS WITH COMING TO TERMS WITH...
I LOST TRACK OF MY FEELINGS.
SINCE HE DIED, IT SEEMS LIKE NOTHING MUCH HAPPENS ANYMORE.

TOO MUCH COFFEE MAN WAS A GREAT GUY. I'M ACTUALLY STARTING TO MISS HIM.
WHAT ARE YOU SAYING?
INTERLUDE
WHY ARE YOU WEARING A PLAIN WHITE T-SHIRT?
BECAUSE I'M SICK OF BEING A BILLBOARD.
TOO MUCH
HOW'S THAT?
THIS SHIRT IS SYMBOLIC OF MY INDIVIDUALITY.
INDIVIDUALITY? WHAT A GREAT IDEA. I THINK I'LL DO THAT TOO.
I'M SAYING- I MISS TOO MUCH COFFEE MAN.
YOU ALWAYS COMPLAINED ABOUT HIM. I THINK THAT YOU DIDN'T EVEN LIKE HIM.
I USED TO LIKE HIM... THEN HE GOT POPULAR...
YOU KNOW HOW HARD IT IS TO LIKE SOMETHING WHEN IT GETS POPULAR.
OF COURSE, NOW THAT HE'S DEAD, IT'S EASY TO LIKE HIM AGAIN.
BUT ONCE HIS DEATH MAKES HIM EVEN MORE POPULAR, I'LL HAVE TO STOP LIKING HIM AGAIN.
AFTER A YEAR OR SO, I CAN START LIKING HIM AGAIN.
I'D DO ANYTHING NOT TO BE TRENDY!

TOO MUCH COFFEE MAN? BUT YOU FELL OUT THAT WINDOW AND WERE KILLED.
I DID! I WAS! BUT LUCKILY THERE WAS A CRACK TEAM OF PARAMEDICS TO REVIVE ME.
WATCH OUT FOR THAT FALLING SAFE!
OH, NO. HE'S DEAD AGAIN.
TOO MUCH COFFEE MAN? YOU'RE ALIVE? HOW? YOU WERE CRUSHED BY THAT FALLING SAFE.
ACTUALLY, I DROPPED THAT SAFE. IT WASN'T ME, BUT MY IMPOSTER TWIN BROTHER WHO FLAB JAB JACKET BLAT
THAT'S NOT TOO MUCH COFFEE MAN. THAT'S A ROBOT.
AND IT'S DYING!
YES! THAT WAS JUST A ROBOT. I SENT IT IN AHEAD OF ME TO MAKE SURE IT'S SAFE. I SEEM TO BE DYING ALL OVER THE PLACE.
I'M COLLECTING THE TOO MUCH COFFEE MAN BODIES IN A PILE OVER HERE.
LOOK OUT! YOU'RE STANDING PRECARIOUSLY CLOSE TO A VERY STEEP AND DANGEROUS STAIRCASE.
OH, NO. HE'S DEAD AGAIN.
SNAP
CRACK
EH. WHATEVER.
HOW CAN YOU SAY THAT?
HE'LL BE BACK.
YOU'RE BACK?
BREAKING YOUR NECK ISN'T AS FATAL AS YOU MIGHT THINK.

I CAN GET USED TO YOU DYING, COMING BACK, DYING, COMING BACK, DYING, COMING BACK, DYING, ETC.

BUT TELL ME...

WHAT'S *IT* LIKE?
WHAT'S *WHAT* LIKE?

WHAT'S IT LIKE TO BE *DEAD*?

WHAT'S IT LIKE? TELL ME! *PLEASE!*

PLEASE PLEASE PLEASE PLEASE PLEASE PLEASE PLEASE PLEASE

OK. I'LL TELL YOU.

BEING DEAD IS—

HUH?
I DON'T GET IT. THERE'S NO PUNCH LINE.
THERE'S NOTHING.
FLIP FLIP FLIP
THERE'S NOTHING.
THAT'S FUNNY. I GUESS.

I THINK I'LL DO A COMIC. IT CAN'T BE THAT HARD. I'LL DO IT ABOUT A GUY SORT OF LIKE ME...AN AVERAGE GUY.
BUY SODA
RELATIONSHIPS, SERIOUS STUFF... REAL LIFE! IT'LL BE GREAT.
BUY BEER
I'M GETTING OLD. I NEED TO START DOING SOMETHING SOON. I'LL START TODAY.
BUY BOOZE
A NEW BEGINNING! A CUT FROM THE PAST!
I NEED A NEW STYLE TOO. I'LL COMMEMORATE MY NEW ATTITUDE WITH A HAIRCUT.
KNOCK
KNOCK
KNOCK
DO YOU WANT TO COME VIDEOTAPE ME GETTING MY HAIR CUT?
SURE. GIVE ME ABOUT FIVE HOURS AND I'LL BE READY.
I WANT TO DO SOMETHING REALLY RADICAL AND SHOCKING, LIKE SHAVING MY HEAD.
OH, HOW SHOCKING.
I DON'T THINK YOU'LL LOOK GOOD WITH YOUR HEAD SHAVED, BUT AT LEAST WE CAN IMMORTALIZE THIS EMBARRASSMENT ON VIDEO.

HERE WE ARE, WATCHING JOEL SHAVE HIS HEAD FOR $12.
THAT'S EVE! THAT'S MY EX-GIRLFRIEND! AND SHE'S HOLDING HANDS WITH SOME OTHER GUY!
THIS IS HORRIBLE!!!
THIS IS GREAT!!!

COFFEE SHOP
I CAN'T BELIEVE SHE'S GOING OUT WITH SOMEONE *ELSE*.
YOU *BROKE UP*!
YOU'RE *NEUROTIC*. YOU NEED TO *MOVE ON* AND OBSESS ON SOMETHING MORE *PRODUCTIVE*.
THE OLDER I GET, THE MORE *NEUROTIC* I BECOME.
I'M *DEPRESSED*, AND I'VE BECOME OBSESSED WITH INJURING MYSELF.
YOU LOOK REALLY *STUPID* WITH YOUR HEAD SHAVED.
WHEN I BICYCLE, I IMAGINE WHAT IT WOULD BE LIKE TO *CRASH*.
YOU LOOK LIKE A FREAKY LITTLE *BIRD*.
WHEN I'M IN A CAR, I THINK ABOUT OPENING THE DOOR AND *JUMPING* OUT.
IT WAS A *MISTAKE* TO SHAVE YOUR HEAD.
WHEN I'M MAKING DINNER, I THINK ABOUT CUTTING OFF A FINGER JUST TO SEE WHAT IT'S LIKE.
I CAN'T TAKE YOU SERIOUSLY.
I REALLY THINK YOU SHOULD HAVE WAITED TO SHAVE YOUR HEAD UNTIL *AFTER* YOU GOT A *NEW* GIRLFRIEND.

I FINISHED WRITING MY SCREENPLAY.
THAT'S COOL... I'M GOING TO DO A COMIC BOOK.
WHY? COMICS ARE STUPID. IT'S A TON OF WORK, AND YOU WON'T MAKE MONEY.
THIS ONE IS POPULAR, THE DRAWING ISN'T GOOD, AND THE IDEAS ARE THINGS THAT I'VE THOUGHT MYSELF.
OF COURSE. "GOOD WRITING IS ABOUT EXPRESSING THE IDEAS THAT ARE OFTEN THOUGHT BUT NOT YET SAID."
AND THAT'S A QUOTE I COULD HAVE MADE UP... BUT DIDN'T.
SCREENPLAYS ARE BETTER. JUST KNOCK OFF A BUNCH OF CLICHÉS AND LET OTHER PEOPLE REWRITE IT TO MAKE IT WORSE. THEN DISAVOW ALL ASSOCIATION. IT'S GREAT.
I LIKE THIS COMIC.
YIKES. I'VE GOT TO GO MEET THIS AGENT GUY. ARE YOU GOING TO BE OK? IT MUST SUCK SEEING YOUR EX-GIRLFRIEND IN LOVE WITH SOMEONE ELSE.
I'M TOTALLY DEPRESSED.
OK. I'LL SEE YOU LATER.
'BYE.
BUY BOOZE
IT CAN'T JUST END LIKE THIS. HEH HEH HEH...
CONT...

WHEN I GET THROUGH THIS COMIC BOOK, I'M GOING TO GO HAVE SOME FUN!!

I'M GOING TO GO SEE SOME MOVIES...

GO DANCING...

READ A BOOK, A REAL BOOK...

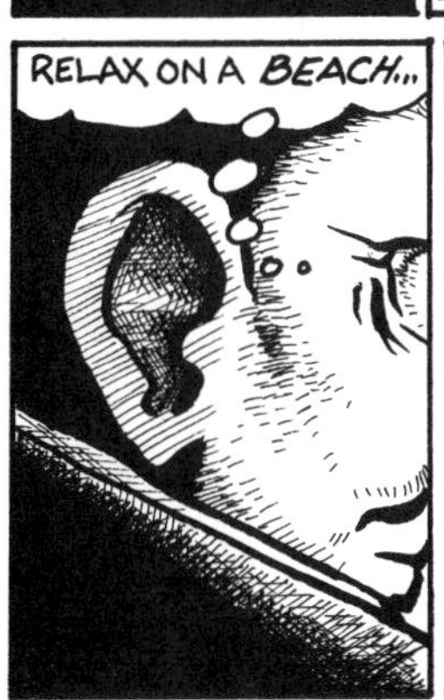
RELAX ON A BEACH...

GO ON A DATE...

ENJOY MY LIFE...

GO HAVE FUN...

FINALLY, FINISHED WITH THIS STUPID COMIC.

GOODBYE, LITTLE COMIC BOOK. I'M TAKING A BREAK.

I CAN'T DO THIS. I HAVE TOO MUCH TO DO–ANOTHER COMIC TO DRAW.

DING DONG

I'M TELLING YOU. *THIS* IS WHERE THE GIRL WHO DRAWS *TOO MUCH COFFEE MAN* LIVES.

YES? HELLO?

UM... ARE YOU THE...UH... *PERSON* WHO DRAWS TOO MUCH COFFEE MAN?

YES. *WHY?*

CAN WE SEE YOUR COMIC BOOK?

SURE. COME ON IN.

I'M WORKING ON *PAGE 112.* I DRAW IT *BIG,* THEN...

DID YOU MAKE A LOT OF *MONEY* FROM THE COMMERCIAL?

UH...

WHY DID YOU DO A COMIC BOOK FROM A COMMERCIAL?

IS IT BECAUSE IT'S SUCH A *COOL* CHARACTER?

YOUR COMIC BOOK IS WORTH MONEY NOW.
IT'S GOING UP IN VALUE.
DO YOU HAVE ANY FIRST PRINTINGS OF NUMBER ONE?
NO. I SOLD ALL OF THEM.
YOU BLEW IT. THOSE ARE WORTH A LOT OF MONEY.
YOU COULD HAVE MADE A LOT OF MONEY.
I'M MORE INTERESTED IN DOING COMICS THAN MAKING A LOT OF MONEY.
YOU MADE A LOT OF MONEY FROM YOUR COMMERCIAL.
YOU LUCKED OUT WITH YOUR GIMMICKY CHARACTER.
YOU WERE SMART TO DO A COFFEE CHARACTER.
COFFEE IS TRENDY.
RING
CAN WE HAVE FREE T-SHIRTS?
IT'LL BE LIKE ADVERTISING.
I GOTTA GET THE PHONE.
RING RING RING
UH... IT'S A FRIEND OF MINE.
WHY DON'T YOU GUYS COME BACK LATER?

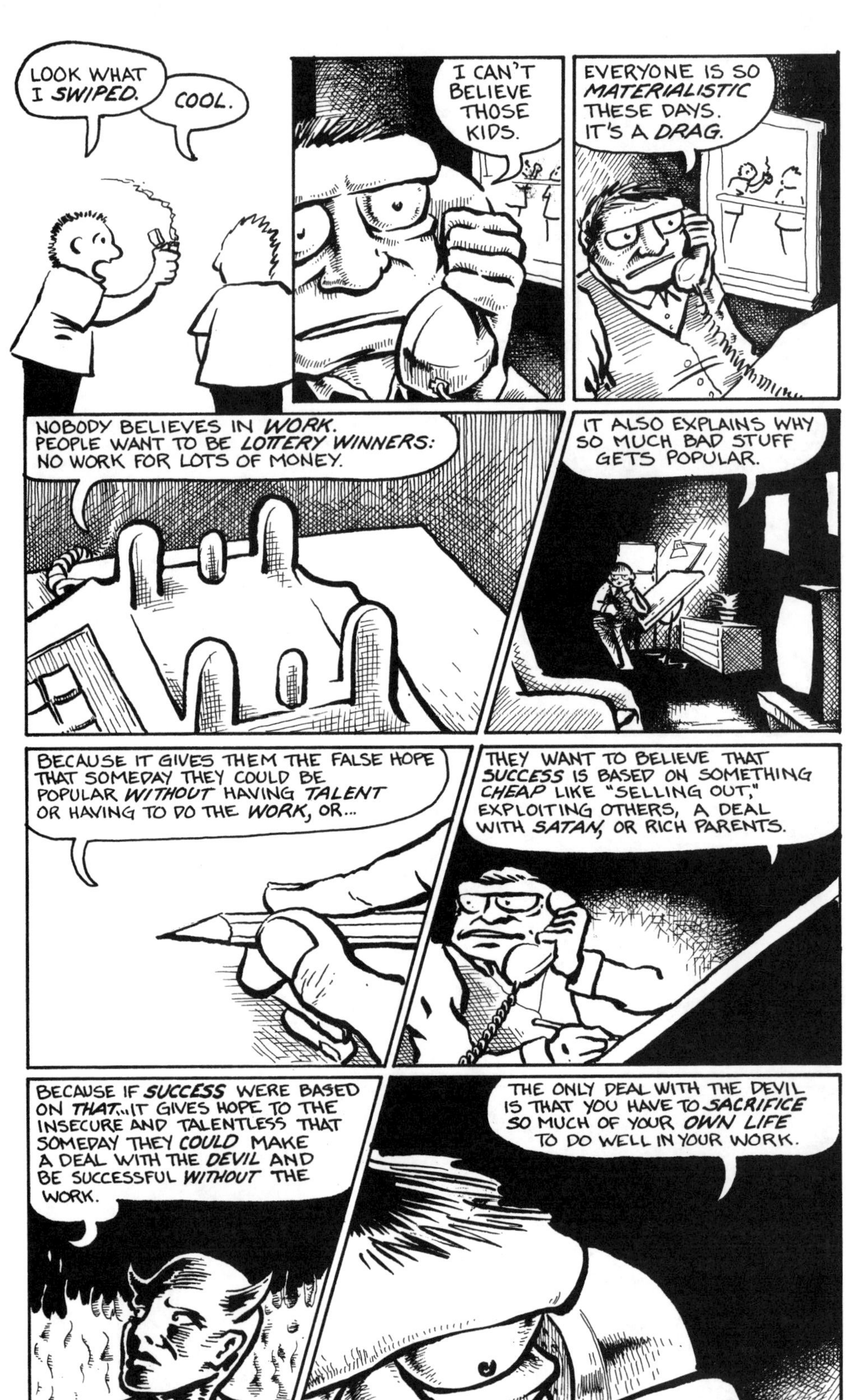
LOOK WHAT I SWIPED.
COOL.
I CAN'T BELIEVE THOSE KIDS.
EVERYONE IS SO MATERIALISTIC THESE DAYS. IT'S A DRAG.
NOBODY BELIEVES IN WORK. PEOPLE WANT TO BE LOTTERY WINNERS: NO WORK FOR LOTS OF MONEY.
IT ALSO EXPLAINS WHY SO MUCH BAD STUFF GETS POPULAR.
BECAUSE IT GIVES THEM THE FALSE HOPE THAT SOMEDAY THEY COULD BE POPULAR WITHOUT HAVING TALENT OR HAVING TO DO THE WORK, OR...
THEY WANT TO BELIEVE THAT SUCCESS IS BASED ON SOMETHING CHEAP LIKE "SELLING OUT," EXPLOITING OTHERS, A DEAL WITH SATAN, OR RICH PARENTS.
BECAUSE IF SUCCESS WERE BASED ON THAT...IT GIVES HOPE TO THE INSECURE AND TALENTLESS THAT SOMEDAY THEY COULD MAKE A DEAL WITH THE DEVIL AND BE SUCCESSFUL WITHOUT THE WORK.
THE ONLY DEAL WITH THE DEVIL IS THAT YOU HAVE TO SACRIFICE SO MUCH OF YOUR OWN LIFE TO DO WELL IN YOUR WORK.

ON *TOO MUCH COFFEE MAN* #6 - #7

When I started working on the 6th issue of *Too Much Coffee Man*, I faced a problem. The time that had passed in reality was very different from the time that had passed in the comic book. It had been a full year since the previous comic book, and I was slated to draw the next week in the comic book.

I could have skipped ahead in the comic-book timeline, made it a year later. But I didn't want to. I had structure in the comics. Each issue the cartoonist would get a little bit more successful, and Joel would fail a little bit more. I wanted an incremental rise and decline (respectively).

I started work on number 6. But it wasn't fun. I wanted to work on the 8th issue. I wanted to wrap up the stories and show Joel living on the street and the cartoonist living the high life. I didn't want to work on all the stuff in between. I wanted to draw the punch line, not the setup.

Slowly I saw that the only way for me to be true to myself was to draw what I wanted to draw, and skip the rest. I thought, "I can't do that; it's against the rules." Then I realized, "What rules? It's my comic book. I don't need to ask permission. After all, it's my supper, and I can eat the dessert first if I want."

Then I saw that this would give me the chance to create the rarest comics ever. There's nothing rarer than not existing. That's when the humor hit me. I imagined people telling me how they loved those issues (the ones that don't exist). I saw fans bugging store owners for the comics that don't exist. It made me laugh.

Then again, maybe people would be mad at me. It's rude to be deceptive. But I've always written my comics with the logic that if I think it's funny, then other people will think it's funny too. You can send the fan letters to me. Send the hate mail to my editor.

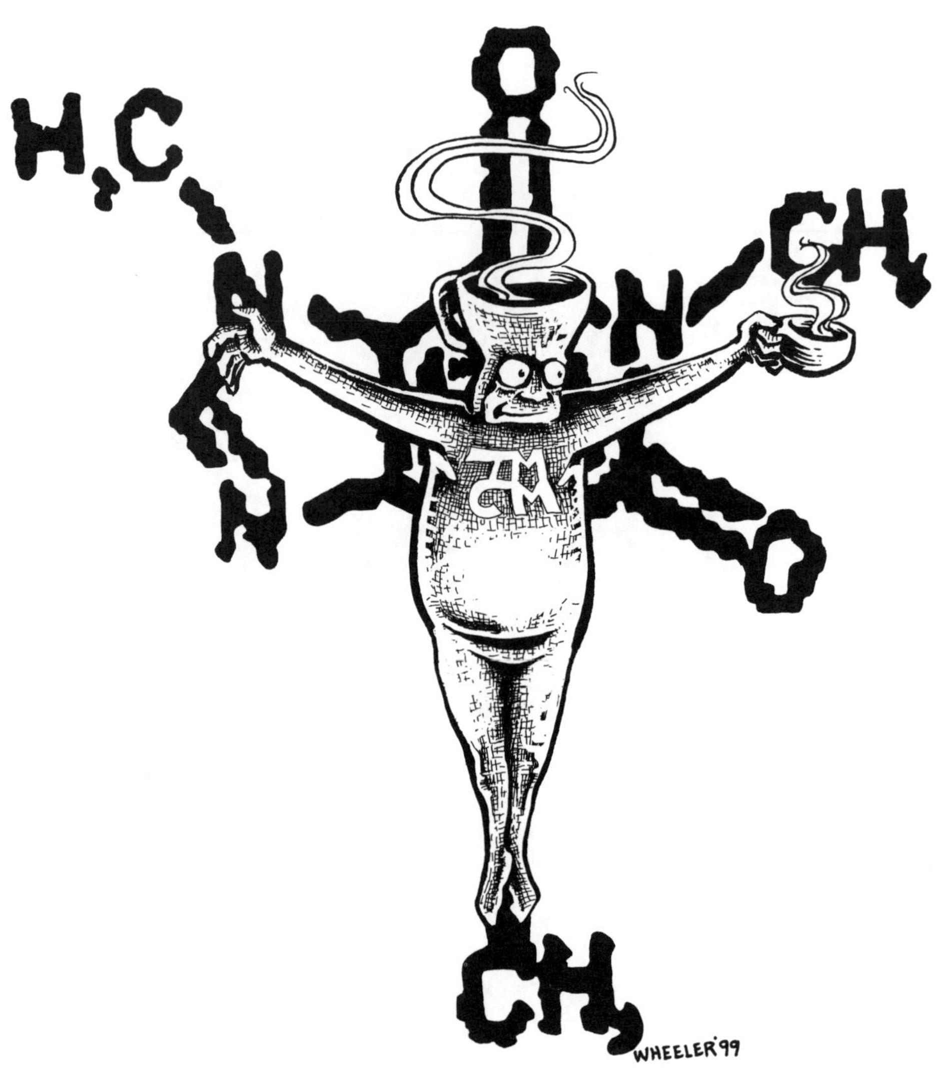
CM
WHEELER'99

I'VE HAD IT UP TO *HERE* WITH *VISUAL METAPHORS.*
1.

THANK YOU FOR THE *RUDE SERVICE.* YOU'VE REALLY COMMUNICATED THAT YOUR JOB IS BENEATH YOU.

TOO MUCH
COFFEE
MAN
GRRRR.
versus
EVERYTHING

I'VE DECIDED TO HATE EVERYTHING! ...AND FIGHT EVERYTHING THAT I HATE!

I'M ANGRY AT THE WORLD!

I'LL PUSH ALL THE BUTTONS IN THIS ELEVATOR!
PUSH
PUSH
PUSH
PUSH

DAMN BUILDING! GRRRRR!

I CURSE THIS TRAFFIC!

STUPID SUNSET!

DUMB WALK HOME.

I HATE MY GOVERNMENT WHEN THEY LIE TO ME.
I HATE MY GOVERNMENT WHEN THEY TELL ME THE TRUTH.

I HATE MY TELEVISION.

I HATE IT WHEN PEOPLE CALL ME.

I HATE IT WHEN PEOPLE DON'T CALL ME.

I HATE MY DISHES FOR BEING DIRTY.

THEY'RE NOT DIRTY ANYMORE.

IT'S EXHAUSTING HATING EVERYTHING.

MY CHILDREN ARE *HUNGRY*, MY WIFE IS *SICK*. WE'RE DESPERATE FOR *MONEY*. THAT LADY HAS MORE MONEY THAN SHE KNOWS WHAT TO DO WITH
AND MY
CAT NEE
TO THE VET.
I TRIED
A REAL JOB
BUT W
MINIMUM
WAG
ENOUGH TO
BUY
OF COFFEE.
I C
ON WELFARE
BUT
SUCKS.

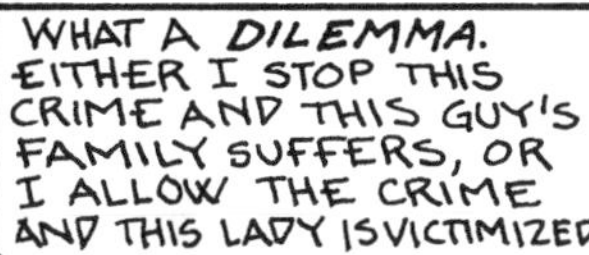

THIS IS ONE OF "THOSE PROBLEMS" THAT CAN ONLY BE SOLVED BY A *FUNDAMENTAL RESTRUCTURING* OF OUR SOCIETY. I COULD ONLY DO THAT IF I WERE

POLLUTION, OVERPOPULATION, UNFAIR DISTRIBUTION OF WEALTH, INTERNATIONAL ENNUI, LONG LINES AT BANKS, BAD TELEVISION, DISEASE, STARVATION, FLOOD, FAMINE, THE HOLE IN THE OZONE LAYER, ENDANGERED SPECIES, BOVINE GROWTH HORMONES AND ANTIBIOTICS THAT PROMOTE PUS IN COW MILK, PEOPLE WHO DON'T HAVE TALENT BUT ARE POPULAR ANYWAY, CROP CIRCLES, HOMELESSNESS AND POVERTY, COMMERCIAL RADIO, CAR ALARMS, LAWN BLOWERS, TAXES, TWO-PARTY POLITICS, PHONE BILLS, BARKING DOGS, PARKING METERS, TRAFFIC, PRODUCT PLACEMENT IN MOVIES, MULTIMEDIA EVENTS, NATURAL DISASTERS, ETHNIC STRIFE, CIVIL UNREST, COLA WARS, BOTTLED WATER, AWKWARD BIRTH CONTROL, JERRY SPRINGER, COPS, MONOPOLIES (NOT THE GAME), LAUGH TRACKS, CAREER COMEBACKS, WITTY REPARTEE, ALL-STAR GAMES, DREAM TEAMS, LONG LISTS OF THINGS THAT ARE WRONG WITH THE WORLD, BUT HE DOESN'T STOP THERE...

ONCE THE *PROBLEMS* OF THE WORLD ARE SOLVED, THE SUPERVILLAINS BANISHED, CRIME ELIMINATED, *TOO MUCH COFFEE MAN* TURNS HIS ATTENTION TO THE *LESSER PROBLEMS*.

HEY, YOU! DON'T CROSS AGAINST THE LIGHT!

SORRY.

EVERYTHING WRONG IS PUT *RIGHT*, AND REALLY GOOD *SOCIAL PROGRAMS* ARE GETTING ADEQUATE FUNDING.

EVERYTHING IS *PERFECT*. ≥YAWN≤

GOOD DOG.

SQUISH

OOOPS.

UNFORTUNATELY, BEING *ALL POWERFUL* CAN LEAD TO *ACCIDENTS*.

SORRY, LITTLE DOG.

I'VE HAD IT ALL. I'VE DONE IT ALL. EVERYONE WORSHIPS ME.

I'M DEPRESSED.

THERE IS NOTHING LEFT TO DO BUT KILL MYSELF.
UNFORTUNATELY, IT'S IMPOSSIBLE TO BE HARMED WHEN YOU ARE INVINCIBLE.
IT DOESN'T EVEN HURT.
BANG

I COULD HANG HERE ALL DAY.
IS THERE NOTHING I CAN DO?

I'LL FLY TO THE CENTER OF THE SUN AND BURN TO DEATH.

I'M NOT EVEN GETTING A TAN.

THE BLACK HOLE IS THE TRASH COMPACTOR OF THE UNIVERSE. I'LL BE SQUASHED LIKE A BUG! IF THIS DOESN'T KILL ME, NOTHING WILL!

NOTHING.

HA HA HA. LOOK, IT'S TOO MUCH COFFEE MAN, THE TRAGIC HERO, WHO'S TOO POWERFUL EVEN TO KILL HIMSELF.
WHAT A RUBE.
THIS MAKES ME MAD!!!
YIKES
I'LL PUSH THE ENTIRE PLANET EARTH INTO THE SUN! LET'S SEE HOW PEOPLE LIKE THAT!
THEN I'LL DESTROY THE SUN!
I'LL SQUISH THE SOLAR SYSTEM!
PUSH
I'LL DESTROY EVERYTHING!
RRIIP
AND THE SOUND OF REALITY ITSELF BEING TORN ASUNDER IS HEARD.

I'VE DESTROYED EVERYTHING.
IT'S ALL GONE.

IT WAS FUN!

I WAS 9 YEARS OLD
AT MY FRIEND'S 10TH
BIRTHDAY PARTY.

IT WAS A *HOT* DAY. EVERYBODY WAS *HAPPY*. THERE WERE A *LOT* OF PRESENTS AND A *TON* OF CAKE. WE HAD BEEN PLAYING BASEBALL ALL AFTERNOON. WE WERE HOT AND TIRED. IT WAS THE END OF THE GAME AND I WAS UP TO BAT.

WE HAD TWO OUTS. WE NEEDED ONE RUN TO WIN. THE BASES WERE LOADED. ANY BASE-HIT WOULD WIN THE GAME FOR US. I WAS NERVOUS, BUT I KNEW IN MY HEART THAT I COULD DO IT.

BUT IT WAS A *FOUL BALL*.
PLOP.

A *FOUL BALL* COUNTED AS A *STRIKE*. IT MADE SENSE–BUILD THE *SUSPENSE*. I HAD *EVERYBODY'S* ATTENTION. MY TEAM WAS YELLING *ENCOURAGEMENTS*, THEIR TEAM WAS YELLING *INSULTS*. IT WAS NOISY.

I MADE *ANOTHER STRIKE*, AND THE PRESSURE WAS REALLY ON ME. TWO STRIKES. I WANTED TO HIT THE BALL AS **HARD** AS I COULD, BUT I KNEW THAT *CONTROL* WAS THE KEY.

STRIKE THREE.

GAME OVER.
Hair Today
WE'VE MOVED

EVERY SINGLE THING I'D EVER SEEN ON TELEVISION, UP TO THAT POINT, HAD LED ME TO BELIEVE THAT I WOULD HIT THAT BALL AND BE A HERO.
MUCH

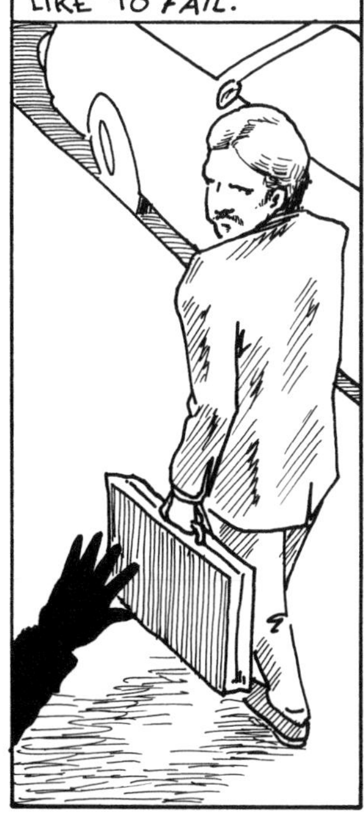
MAYBE A SMALL PART OF MYSELF WAS CURIOUS ABOUT WHAT IT WOULD BE LIKE TO FAIL.

AFTER MY BIG STRIKEOUT, EVERYBODY MADE FUN OF ME. I NEVER PLAYED BASEBALL AGAIN. I JUST WOULDN'T DO IT.

I CAN'T BELIEVE THIS PLACE CLOSED DOWN. I USED TO *LOVE* COMING HERE. IT'S AS GOOD A PLACE AS ANY TO LIGHT UP.

IS *THAT* WHO I *THINK* IT IS? *YIKES!* HE LOOKS *TERRIBLE*.

JOEL?

TRIXIE?

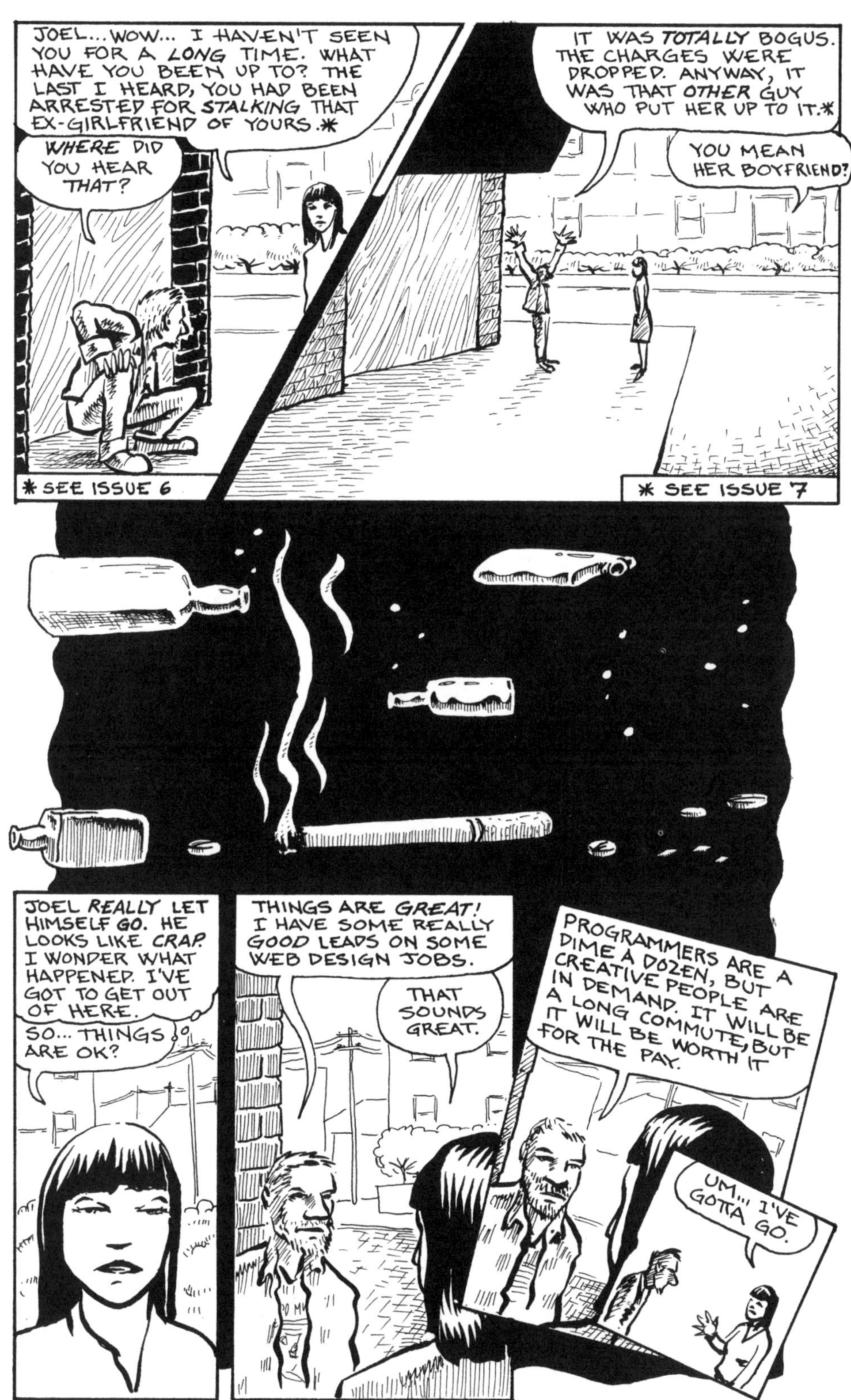
JOEL... WOW... I HAVEN'T SEEN YOU FOR A LONG TIME. WHAT HAVE YOU BEEN UP TO? THE LAST I HEARD, YOU HAD BEEN ARRESTED FOR STALKING THAT EX-GIRLFRIEND OF YOURS.*
WHERE DID YOU HEAR THAT?
* SEE ISSUE 6
IT WAS TOTALLY BOGUS. THE CHARGES WERE DROPPED. ANYWAY, IT WAS THAT OTHER GUY WHO PUT HER UP TO IT.*
YOU MEAN HER BOYFRIEND?
* SEE ISSUE 7
JOEL REALLY LET HIMSELF GO. HE LOOKS LIKE CRAP. I WONDER WHAT HAPPENED. I'VE GOT TO GET OUT OF HERE.
SO... THINGS ARE OK?
THINGS ARE GREAT! I HAVE SOME REALLY GOOD LEADS ON SOME WEB DESIGN JOBS.
THAT SOUNDS GREAT.
PROGRAMMERS ARE A DIME A DOZEN, BUT CREATIVE PEOPLE ARE IN DEMAND. IT WILL BE A LONG COMMUTE, BUT IT WILL BE WORTH IT FOR THE PAY.
UM... I'VE GOTTA GO.

WE SHOULD GO GET A BEER SOMETIME.
SURE. SOUNDS GREAT. I'LL SEE YOU LATER.
WHAT A LOSER.
'BYE.
I HOPE THAT WASN'T THE FORESHADOWING FOR MY HIGH SCHOOL REUNION.
SHE LOOKS GREAT. I SHOULD GO OUT WITH HER.
I DON'T EVEN HAVE ENOUGH MONEY FOR A BEER. AT LEAST I HAVE SMOKES.
I SHOULD HAVE ASKED HER FOR SOME MONEY.

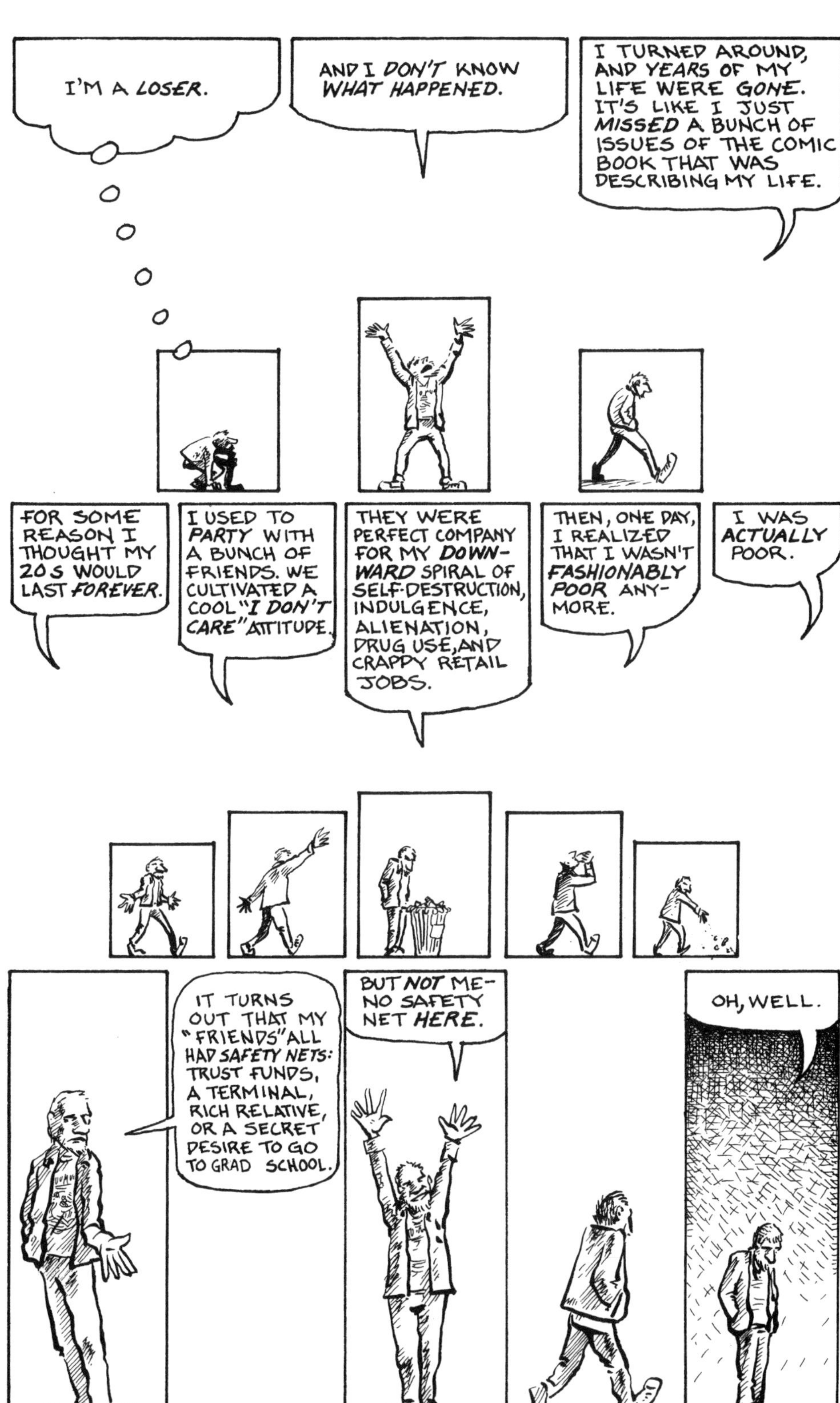
I'M A LOSER.
AND I DON'T KNOW WHAT HAPPENED.
I TURNED AROUND, AND YEARS OF MY LIFE WERE GONE. IT'S LIKE I JUST MISSED A BUNCH OF ISSUES OF THE COMIC BOOK THAT WAS DESCRIBING MY LIFE.
FOR SOME REASON I THOUGHT MY 20S WOULD LAST FOREVER.
I USED TO PARTY WITH A BUNCH OF FRIENDS. WE CULTIVATED A COOL "I DON'T CARE" ATTITUDE.
THEY WERE PERFECT COMPANY FOR MY DOWNWARD SPIRAL OF SELF-DESTRUCTION, INDULGENCE, ALIENATION, DRUG USE, AND CRAPPY RETAIL JOBS.
THEN, ONE DAY, I REALIZED THAT I WASN'T FASHIONABLY POOR ANYMORE.
I WAS ACTUALLY POOR.
IT TURNS OUT THAT MY "FRIENDS" ALL HAD SAFETY NETS: TRUST FUNDS, A TERMINAL, RICH RELATIVE, OR A SECRET DESIRE TO GO TO GRAD SCHOOL.
BUT NOT ME- NO SAFETY NET HERE.
OH, WELL.

WHEN DO I
START FEELING
SUCCESSFUL?

MAYBE WHEN I MAKE MORE MONEY.
I'M MAKING MORE MONEY THAN I EVER HAVE IN MY WHOLE LIFE. IT ISN'T MONEY.
RECOGNITION?
I WON THOSE TWO AWARDS* WHICH MADE ME HAPPY... FOR A BIT. AND THE ARTICLES ABOUT ME HAVE BEEN TOTALLY FLATTERING.
*SEE ISSUE 6
FANS?
MY COMIC BOOK SELLS REALLY WELL. AND I GET LOTS OF FAN MAIL. PLENTY OF PEOPLE SEEM TO APPRECIATE MY WORK. I SHOULD BE HAPPY.
I SHOULD BE HAPPY: BUT I HAVE THE SAME EXACT INSECURITIES I HAD WHEN I STARTED DRAWING COMICS.
TAXI
AM I GOING TO BE PLAGUED WITH SELF-DOUBT MY WHOLE LIFE? MAYBE I SHOULD WORK HARDER.

COULD YOU DO A SKETCH FOR MY GIRLFRIEND?

SURE.

I'M DRAWING *MYSELF* DRAWING *TOO MUCH COFFEE MAN.*

YOU DON'T *LOOK* LIKE HOW YOU *DRAW* YOURSELF.

IT'S AN *EMOTIONAL* SELF-PORTRAIT.

I'M TRYING TO DRAW MY OWN COMIC BOOK. I WISH I COULD DRAW MORE, BUT I HAVE TO MAKE MONEY AT MY *DAY JOB.*

I KNOW WHAT YOU MEAN.

I STEP OUT OF THE COMIC STORE, AND I I STEP FROM *MODERATE FAME* TO *TOTAL ANONYMITY.*

COMICS 'N' JUNK

HELLO, IS ART THERE?

YEP. IT'S OVER.

IT WENT BETTER THAN I EXPECTED.

I'M READY FOR A BEER.

SUPER. I'LL SEE YOU SOON.

I USED TO WALK EVERYWHERE BECAUSE I *DIDN'T* HAVE A CAR. *NOW* I WALK SO I CAN WORK OFF THE *FAT* I GOT FROM WORKING *TOO MUCH* SO I COULD BUY A CAR.

WHY IS ART *ALWAYS* LATE?

I NEED *GLASSES*. IS *THAT* ART? IT'S *GOT* TO BE HIM. BUT WHO IS HE TALKING TO?

HE'S *SCAMMING* ON THAT GIRL... WHAT AN *OPPORTUNIST*. BUT, THEN AGAIN, *I'M* THE ONE WHO'S SITTING *ALONE*.

HEY, *ART*!

WHAT'S HE *DOING*? IS HE GETTING HER *PHONE NUMBER*?

SORRY I'M LATE. HAVE YOU BEEN HERE LONG?
NOT REALLY.

WHO'S THE GIRL?
I JUST MET HER. SHE'S CUTE, ISN'T SHE?

I DON'T KNOW *HOW* YOU DO IT.
IT'S *EASY*. I PRETEND THAT I'M *NOT* LONELY.

HERE WE ARE: TWO FAMOUS CARTOONISTS, HANGING OUT AND DRINKING BEER. WANNA DRAW?
NO WAY! I'M OFF DUTY.
WHEN YOU DRINK BEER, DOES EVERYONE MAKE THE SAME JOKE ABOUT HOW YOU SHOULD BE DRINKING COFFEE?
I WISH PEOPLE WOULD DISTINGUISH ME FROM MY WORK.
HOW IS YOUR WORK GOING, ANYWAY?
GOOD. BUT I SPEND WAY TOO MUCH TIME ON BUSINESS AND PROMOTION. I FEEL LIKE I DRAW MY COMIC BOOK IN MY SPARE TIME.
ESPECIALLY NOW, WITH MY ANIMATION THING, I HAVE EVEN LESS TIME FOR DRAWING.
I HEARD THAT YOU HAVE A CARTOON DEAL IN THE WORKS.
I WAS OFFERED A DEAL, BUT I DIDN'T TAKE IT. THEY WANTED TO OWN EVERYTHING.
I KNOW I'M BEING RUDE, BUT I'M CURIOUS... HOW MUCH DID THEY OFFER?
A MILLION.
WHAT?

I CAN'T BELIEVE THAT YOU WERE OFFERED A MILLION BUCKS FOR YOUR COMIC AND YOU TURNED IT DOWN!

YOU COULD ACTUALLY BE A MILLIONARE!

YOU COULD RETIRE AND LIVE OFF THE INTEREST!

YOU COULD SELL OUT AND START A NEW COMIC.

NO OFFENSE, BUT YOU HAVE MORE INTEGRITY THAN I GAVE YOU CREDIT FOR.

AREN'T YOU TEMPTED TO TAKE THEIR MONEY?
NOT REALLY... ARE YOU READY TO LEAVE?

HOW CAN YOU NOT BE TEMPTED?
I CAN GET MORE.

I CAN'T DECIDE IF I'VE LOST ALL RESPECT FOR YOU, OR IF I RESPECT YOU MORE.

SPARE CHANGE?
NO. SORRY.
THAT BUM WAS WEARING A TOO MUCH COFFEE MAN SHIRT.
WEIRD.
A MILLION?
YEP.
END.

AFTERWORD

When I was nine, I had the insight that aging was dying. I realized that I would never be the same person that I was at that moment. The nine-year-old Shannon would be dead and replaced by the twelve-year-old Shannon. Therefore the nine-year-old me would soon be dead.

I didn't see any escape from my mortality. The best I could do was to live on in my own memory. I promised myself that I would remember what it was like to stand there in that doorway, next to the light switch, watching the dust floating in and out of the shaft of sunlight that came through the window. I would remember the melancholy I felt as a nine-year-old pondering the future.

The indicia in every comic book states that all references to persons, places, etc. are purely coincidental. There couldn't be a bigger lie. The situations are as accurate as I could make them. The feelings are real. The characters are my friends.

I read these comics and I remember who I was.

— Shannon Wheeler

TOO MUCH COFFEE MAN'S™

PARADE OF TIRADE

created, written, & drawn by
SHANNON WHEELER

cover sculpture by
BRIAN KLAUS

editor • DIANA SCHUTZ
production • RICH POWERS
book design • CARY GRAZZINI
publisher • MIKE RICHARDSON

This book collects issues 1-8 of TOO MUCH COFFEE MAN, published by Adhesive Comics.

Address all correspondence to:
Adhesive Comics
P.O. Box 14549
Portland, OR 97293-0549

www.TMCM.com
www.TooMuchCoffeeMan.com

Published by
Dark Horse Comics, Inc.
10956 SE Main Street
Milwaukie, OR 97222

First edition: November 1999
ISBN: 1-56971-437-1

1 3 5 7 9 10 8 6 4 2
PRINTED IN CANADA